THE LITTLE BOOK OF
THRIFTY FIXES FOR THE HOME

THE LITTLE BOOK OF
THRIFTY
FIXES
FOR THE
HOME

BRIDGET BODOANO

QUADRILLE

editorial director Jane O'Shea
creative director Helen Lewis
project editor Hilary Mandleberg
designer Claire Peters
illustrator Bridget Bodoano
production director Vincent Smith
production controller Ruth Deary

First published in 2008 by
Quadrille Publishing

Text and illustrations ©
2008 Bridget Bodoano
Design and layout © 2008
Quadrille Publishing Ltd

Library of Congress Cataloging-in-Publication Data

Bodoano, Bridget.
  The little book of thrifty fixes for the home / Bridget
Bodoano.
    p. cm.
  Includes index.
  ISBN 978-1-84400-631-1 (pbk.)
  1. Interior decoration--Economic aspects. I. Title.
  NK2113.B67 2008
  643.7--dc22

                                    2007048951

ISBN 978-1-84400-596-3

Printed in Singapore

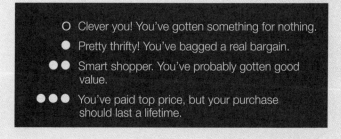

O   Clever you! You've gotten something for nothing.

●   Pretty thrifty! You've bagged a real bargain.

●● Smart shopper. You've probably gotten good
    value.

●●● You've paid top price, but your purchase
    should last a lifetime.

It's smart to be thrifty. For some time now the ultra-fashionable have been wearing secondhand, and even top designers are to be seen scouring thrift shops for ideas. But keeping up with trends is exhausting—to say nothing of the effect on your bank balance—so prudent people are looking to moderate their desires. Reasons to be thrifty vary from wanting to be stylish on a restricted budget to a rejection of materialism, an acknowledgment of the need to cut down on consumption for the sake of the planet, and a wish to spend money differently and with different priorities.

This means that thrift is not just about spending less; it's also about buying less and, when you do spend, spending wisely and using flair and imagination, rather than money, to get the look. In a world where retail has become a leisure activity, it's difficult not to be tempted by all the goodies for sale, especially when many of them are so cheap. But the days of the throwaway society are numbered, and it's becoming harder to ignore the fact that rampant consumerism is unsustainable and that we have to change our habits, curb our enthusiasms, buy what we need, rather than what we want, and learn to appreciate the value of quality above quantity.

All this may sound horribly puritanical but it doesn't mean that shopping can't be fun. Far from it. The challenge of finding a real bargain in the form of an expensive grown-up item at a reduced price, or a well-designed, well-made, but inexpensive gem, together with the challenge of buying stuff that you really love and will want to keep for years rather than weeks, can provide even the most dedicated shopaholic with the necessary buzz.

Whether you're strapped for cash on the way up or are downshifting to a simpler existence, a thrifty approach can help to save you not only money but time, energy, and, possibly, your sanity, too.

Bridget Bodoano

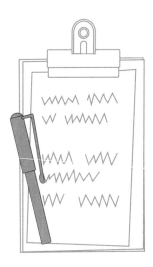

1 thrifty principles

what's this thing called **thrift**?

Thrift isn't about spending less; it's about spending wisely. We've all, at some time, bought a lot of cheap stuff that, if we're honest, turned out to be a waste of money. If we added up the cost of everything that didn't live up to our expectations, we'd find that, for the same money, we could have bought the thing we really coveted but didn't buy in the first place because it was too expensive. So thrift isn't penny-pinching and deprivation; it's getting the most for your money, using wit and wisdom, and having fun at the same time.

thrifty principles

reasons to be thrifty
1 **to save money**

We aren't all in a highly paid job; and for many of us, money is tight. On top of that, our fast-moving, ever-changing world means that economic uncertainty might strike at any time. And sometimes a change of circumstances—like the arrival of a new baby or a change of job—can entail a bit of belt-tightening, too.

If you avoid the pressure of "keeping up," it will help you to keep debt down. And who knows? Taking a thrifty approach can save you money to use for vacations, keeping fit, culture, entertainment, and hobbies. It could even allow you to invest in learning and retraining—which could lead to a better job or could just help you rethink your priorities.

reasons to be thrifty
2 **for a better lifestyle**

The dictionary definition of thrift mentions frugality, which may sound rather puritanical. However, limiting your financial commitments and downshifting is no longer seen as failure but is acknowledged by many as a better, more liberating way of living. What's more, it's not a bad idea to stop and reevaluate your life from time to time. Personal circumstances change, as do ambitions and aspirations.

reasons to be thrifty
3 **for the sake of the planet**

The world needs to be thrifty in its use of resources, for these are rapidly becoming depleted as a result, partly, of rampant consumerism (see pages 288–289).

reasons to be thrifty
4 **because it's in fashion**

Conspicuous consumerism is no longer as cool as it was in the nineties, and there's no longer any stigma attached to buying secondhand. Instead, suddenly, it's smart to be thrifty. Just watch the "fashionistas." For some time, they've been wearing secondhand clothes, and top designers have been seen scouring thrift shops for garments not only to wear but also as a source of ideas. Now old is the new "new," and pursuing a thrifty lifestyle is very "à la mode."

last word

Think positively and imaginatively—readjusting your aspirations to bring them into line with your income doesn't have to mean exchanging designer labels and meals out for sackcloth and gruel.

2 **thrifty** style

chain store to **chic**

The material things in life cost money, but style is free. The smartest people achieve stylishness through a combination of prudence and panache, somehow managing to turn chain store finds into high fashion and secondhand into swish and swanky. Follow the rules, add a dash of imagination, and you'll have a look that suits your home and your bank balance.

magazine **know-how**

All the magazines tell us how to put together our own style of dressing, using a mixture of chain-store and designer labels plus a few choice accessories, so why not use the very same approach when it comes to dressing up your home?

strength in numbers

A cheap item on its own draws attention to itself and can look cheap, but it gains confidence in a group. Take inexpensive bookcases, for example. These are remarkable value but look much more convincing— and more costly—when several are lined up in a row.

less is **more**

■ While the more extreme examples of minimalism have been eschewed in favor of practicality and comfort, architect Mies van der Rohe's philosophy of "less is more" lives on in today's fashion for paring down, which has succeeded in introducing a new, simpler feel to our home furnishings and decoration.

■ So, remember that one or two good-looking items will always look better than a motley assortment of the not-so-nice.

■ You also need to realize that when there are fewer objects in a room, more attention is focused on their surroundings. So make sure the backdrop stands up to scrutiny by getting walls, floors, and woodwork into tip-top condition.

LESS COSTS LESS
And finally, remember that less costs less.

 thrifty style

DID YOU KNOW THAT...?

. . . to create an illusion of space and a "light and airy" feel, you should

- use light colors in the home;

- choose furniture that's raised above the floor on legs or even just on casters;

- think horizontally and keep the furniture all one height. A hodgepodge of different heights won't give you those desirable clean lines.

be **inspired**

Look to the top fashion labels for color inspiration and, if you dare, take your paint charts into the fashion boutiques to match up the latest shades. Stores often display clothes grouped in families of colors and tones, as well as patterns and textures. Note how the clothes are accessorized with splashes of other colors. Now go home and use what you've learned to put together a color palette that can form the basis of your own interior scheme.

DID YOU KNOW THAT...?

. . . clever use of color can make the prosaic look sophisticated, can harmonize a chaotic house, can draw together a motley collection of furnishings, and, if necessary, can detract from the imperfect.

. . . using too many different materials will look messy, even if they are expensive, so obeying the rules of good design and keeping to a restricted palette is even more important for thrifty interior decorators.

. . . if you want a classy look, choose muted neutrals such as taupe, warm grays, pale gray-greens, and sage green; and instead of unforgiving pure white, think ivory or bone.

. . . you should avoid primary colors because the cheap versions are rarely good, but if you want to make a bold statement, go for fruity hues such as canteloupe, tangerine, strawberry pink, banana yellow, or a refreshing squeeze of lime.

. . . sugary pastels really don't cut the mustard. Instead choose colors with a cashmere aura—soft, pale pinks, blues, and greens.

. . . if you want dark color, go for charcoal gray, not black, and think rich, deep purples and reds, and matte cobalt blue.

BE OUTRAGEOUS
Add some character to a pleasant but plain house by going mad with outrageous color. If you're feeling bold, paint a whole room. Otherwise adopt the "just one wall" strategy.

up-to-date **accessorizing**

Smart people transform last year's clothes into this season's look with a few carefully chosen accessories. Likewise, a few well-chosen extras can lift, enhance, or detract from the shortcomings of a dull piece of furniture or the listlessness of a tired room.

● **TAKE COVER**
A new throw pillow cover in this season's colors will demonstrate your keen eye for what's "now" and will save you the trouble and expense of going for a complete makeover.

● **FIRM THINGS UP**
Neat, firm cushions and bolsters will pull together a saggy sofa and make it look much more appealing.

● **THROWAWAYS**
Shawls and throws over a sofa or chair can do the trick, but avoid the "bedspread" look. Use layers of smaller throws, and mix tones and textures.

●●● **LEATHER LUXURY**
Just as a beautiful, good-quality handbag or belt can make a chain store suit look a million dollars, so a

thrifty style

single leather chair, footstool, or even just a cushion will lend an impression of quality to a room. Keep to classic colors: tans, creams, and dark browns all look chic and expensive.

●● ART ATTACK

A stunning piece of art, ceramic, or sculpture will be the focus of attention and add zest to a simply furnished room. Seek out new talent at affordable prices at art school thesis exhibitions, art fairs, and local galleries, or be brave and display your own creations, or those of your nearest and dearest.

●●● ONE BIG SPLURGE

If you can't afford to furnish your whole house with the latest designs or the most elegant antiques, invest in a single fine piece, and make it the star attraction. For example, try a stunning chair, ornate mirror, or extravagant bed. Or put an intriguing piece of sculpture in the hall or some custom-made stained glass in your smallest window. Indulge and enjoy.

picture style

CLIP-FRAME GLAMOUR

Clip frames have a tendency to look cheap, so glam them up by matting the picture within a large border on special paper. Try handmade, textured papers or very beautiful art paper.

ONE FRAME SUITS ALL

Sticking to a single style of frame will unify a mixture of prints, paintings, and photographs.

OFF THE WALL

Standing pictures on the floor and propping them against the wall gives you a different vantage point and avoids making holes in the wall. This is really useful for covering plugs, cables, and unsightly floor-level holes or stains.

OLD PRINTS

Look in secondhand bookstores and specialist art booksellers for old exhibition catalogues. These are usually very cheap and are full of good-quality reproductions that you can frame.

SINGLE LINE

A single row of pictures set halfway up the wall looks sophisticated. You don't have to keep to one size, but hang them with all their tops or their bottoms aligned.

WELL PLANNED

A satisfying arrangement of pictures takes time and a great deal of trial and error. You could try using the drawing program on your PC to plot the positions of pictures on a scale drawing and so save your wall from unnecessary holes.

SHELF LIFE

A narrow shelf is a great way to display pictures. Now widely available in wood or metal, they avoid the need for hanging; just prop up the pictures on the shelf and change them around whenever you like.

PLAIN + SIMPLE
Simple aluminum or black frames look very discreet and are the perfect solution for framing black-and-white photographs or drawings.

SIGHT LINES
Don't hang pictures too high, or you won't be able to appreciate them properly. Work out the best viewing position from both a seated and a standing viewpoint.

KEEP CONTROL
Don't dot pictures around the place. Lining them up in disciplined rows or containing them on just one wall has far greater impact.

the **wow**! factor

■ There's no need to hide your peculiar passions or apologize for any eccentric or obsessive tendencies. Bring out those quirky collections, and display them with pride.

■ Whether it's stamps, toy robots, china dogs, model aeroplanes, beer mats, or even shoes, a personal collection has the potential to be the center of attention and to add a touch of wow! to a dull room.

■ An edited selection looks chic, but why not go that little bit further and cover an entire wall with a display using shelves or glass-fronted cabinets? They don't need to match.

find **your** style

Sticking to one design style to create a Mission-style idyll or a Pop Art pad will naturally pull a room together, but be careful it doesn't look stilted, mannered, or just plain boring. Allow beautiful and distinctive items to take center stage by mixing them with plainer, more understated pieces.

delightful **dilapidation**

Long fashionable in Britain, the decorating ethos known as "shabby chic" is now beginning to be taken up by Americans. The name says it all, really—furniture and furnishings are old and a bit worn; walls may have chipped paint or peeling wallpaper. It's a lived-in look, which can appear in various guises, ranging from romantic rustic to remembered retro.

Over time, garish colors can fade into sophistication and a bit of battering can be character building, but shabby chic isn't always as simple as it appears. It requires a dispassionate eye to distinguish between the potentially delightful and the downright dismal.

A few rules apply. If something is of good quality and good design, it will probably maintain its dignity when it's in a state of poor repair. Age rarely gives beauty to anything cheap and ugly or inherently horrible. Cleanliness is also important (see pages 122–125). Freshly laundered threadbare fabrics are soft and charming, but a tacky sofa or rug loses its charm if it's accompanied by anything sticky or crusty. The same goes for chipped paintwork. This looks good only if it's given a thorough wash.

DID YOU KNOW THAT...?

. . . it's possible to make new look old with special paint techniques (see "crackle glaze" and "distressing," page 239) or simply by using old fabrics and coverings and traditional colors and finishes on furnishings, walls, and floors.

. . . some new furniture and furnishings come already distressed, but not all look the part, so be discriminating, and make sure the effect is convincing.

shabby **favorites**

OLD PLAID WOOL BLANKETS
Look for these in grungy browns, muted pinks, and greens. Honeycomb and tapestry blankets, which were much favored in the 1960s and were sold in craft shops and woolen mills, are also back in favor.

CROCHET BLANKETS, SHAWLS, AND PILLOWS
These look charming. An afghan made of granny squares will lend a nostalgic touch to a sofa.

OLD PATCHWORK + QUILTED BEDCOVERS
The more faded the better, and don't worry if the insides are poking through.

CANDLEWICK BEDSPREADS
Once considered horribly "square," but today they're most definitely "now."

BIG, SAGGY ARMCHAIRS

One big saggy armchair will make a strong shabby chic statement (more than one is overdoing it). The leather versions are rather special, but they're becoming increasingly hard to find at affordable prices.

FADED CHINTZ

Keep an eye open for old draperies and sofa and chair covers made from this perennially favorite fabric.

METALWORK

Metal garden furniture, wirework plant holders, and odds and ends. A touch of rust adds character.

SMALL PAINTED BOOKCASES + SHELVES

A nostalgic alternative to smart shelving.

FADED PICTURES IN STOUT WOODEN FRAMES

These can include old sepia photographs picked up at market stalls. They offer a chance to adopt your own ancestors.

bo**hemian style**

Indulging in a little maximalism is the perfect way to achieve big impact on a small budget. It's also a wonderful excuse to rebel against the de-cluttering police. Use throws, rugs, and wall hangings in an array of dangerously dark, rich colors, and sumptuous fabrics and with an adventurous spirit, and you can create an interior that will suit many moods and associations – from the excitement of the souk to the lure of Africa and the exoticism of the British Raj.

What's more, with plenty of dhurries and throws, no one need know that a truly horrible sofa or disgusting carpet lurks underneath. But use a discriminating, discerning eye, or you might end up with a somewhat too convincing imitation of a student bedroom.

HAPPY HIPPY BOHEMIAN
Essentially bare and simple but with a sprinkling of Indian bedspreads, wall hangings, pretty glass lamps, big floor cushions, and lots of candles.

SPICED-UP BOHEMIAN

Features oriental carpets, rugs, kilims, dhurries, rich embroideries, jewel-colored walls and fabrics, plus a selection of ethnic objects, such as large baskets and pots and highly decorative, carved wooden beds, cabinets, tables, and stools.

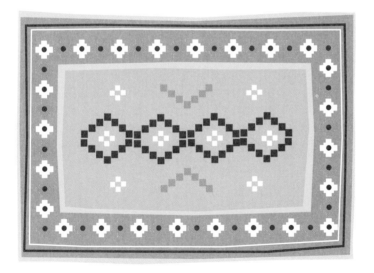

textiles for the bohemian look

INDIAN COTTON BEDSPREADS

Solid-colored and patterned, and still to be found in ethnic shops and markets. They're great for covering sofas, chairs, tables, and beds and can also be used as curtains.

AFRICAN PRINTS

Scour markets and specialist stores for lengths of fantastically colorful printed fabric, which can be used for everything from covers to curtains.

COTTON DHURRIES + KILIMS

Plentiful in chain stores, markets, and discount warehouses, these include everything from bright, bold stripes to subtle traditional patterns. Some are quite small, so go for layers. Okay on the floor, but light colors soon look grubby. Good to hang at windows or on walls or for covering furniture.

ORIENTAL-STYLE CARPETS

Pseudo-oriental carpets bought from markets and bargain outlets are sometimes thin. Choose the best colors, and layer them for a more convincing effect.

EMBROIDERED FABRICS

Shops that stock inexpensive imports will usually carry a selection of embroidered Moroccan-style fabrics. Use them for covers, pillows, wall hangings, and pure decoration.

SARIS

Take advantage of the colors and rich embroidery of traditional sari fabric. They make fabulous curtains or hangings around a bed.

"bloomsbury" style

Take your inspiration from "Charleston," the Sussex home of Duncan Grant and Vanessa Bell, who were members of the famous Bloomsbury Group, in England. They painted their walls, doors, floors, fireplaces, furniture, and screens with exuberant patterns and figures. This thrifty way of turning the ordinary into the extraordinary can best be achieved if you possess more than a dab of artistic talent. But even if you don't, you could use a stencil and limit yourself to decorating a simple item such as a table or the doors of a small cabinet.

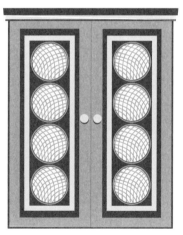

boudoir **style**

Another opportunity for a little opulence is in the boudoir—now making a comeback as a refuge for busy women, where they can reengage with their feminine side. Indulge in silks and satins, lace and velvet, fringed shawls and pretty furnishings, including chaises longues and glamorous dressing tables complete with stool and silver-backed hairbrushes.

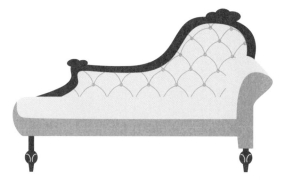

natural **harmony**

The chemical-rich, highly charged atmosphere of our technological age is at odds with our human origins, so it's not surprising that many of us are leaving town and opting for country living. Of those left behind, many aspire to a simpler life, inspired by nature and the countryside. Space, simplicity, order, balance, and harmony are important ingredients, while surrounding ourselves with colors and materials derived directly from nature helps us reconnect with that world, relax, and become reenergized.

■ Raw materials, including unpainted wood and stone, and natural fibers, such as cotton, linen, and wool, all have an intrinsically harmonious quality and so work well together to impart a calm feel in a room.

■ Vegetable dyes, instead of harsh chemical dyes, and shapes that are rounded instead of sharp all help to induce an aura of calm.

■ A calm atmosphere is also created by paying attention to the quality of the light, whether by filtering it through fine cotton curtains or wooden venetian blinds, or by arranging lamps so that they provide pools of light, rather than strong allover illumination.

■ Keep things simple, with not too much to distract the eye or the brain.

■ Follow Zen principles by taking pleasure in the rituals of everyday actions, such as cooking and cleaning, and by enjoying the beauty of everyday objects such as smooth wooden bowls, simple white ceramics—even a favorite knife and chopping board.

back to nature
color inspiration

Think of your favorite places to create
a color scheme inspired by nature.

THE BEACH
Dream of pebble and driftwood grays, sea blues, and greens, plus the warm colors of sand and shingle.

WOODS + FORESTS
These contain mossy and pale leaf greens, loamy browns, and, in fall, brilliant reds, oranges, and golds.

GREEN FIELDS + HEDGEROWS
This landscape offers a myriad shades, including the sharp green of spring grass and early shoots, the fuzzy greens of hayfields, and the speckled green of meadows blotched with wildflowers.

MOUNTAINS
Imagine the textured gray of bare rock, stones, and scrunchy scree, orange lichen, yellow broom, gentle heather purples, and deep green conifers.

THE ORCHARD + THE VEGETABLE PLOT
Here, apples, pears, peaches, and apricots are enriched with the deeper tones of raspberries, strawberries, cherries, and blueberries. For a palette that is marvellously mellow, add milky orange carrots, eggplants, pea greens, and the speckled browns and purples of beans.

modern**(ism)**

The traditional concept of "modern" is one of simple shapes, clean lines, and pared-down interiors with little or no decoration; but some people are now reacting against this extreme form of modernism and are in favor of a more comfortable and characterful look, which includes color, curves, pattern, and texture.

economy modern

Modern is usually chic and expensive, but economy modern can be cooked up using inexpensive lookalike ingredients picked off the shelves of the furniture superstores, used sparingly and arranged carefully in a crisp, clean setting.

tips for getting the
modern look

KEEP IT SIMPLE

Don't overcrowd a room, and don't use too many different styles and designs. Stick to simple geometric shapes. The occasional gentle curve is permissible, but absolutely no twiddly decorative trims.

BARE MINIMUM

Keep floors and walls plain. Bare wooden, stone, or tiled floors are great, and so is rubber, but this is expensive. Paint imperfect floors, or cover them with plain carpet and rugs.

HIDE IT AWAY

"Modern" is now synonymous with "uncluttered," so storage is important. Keep your possessions under control and preferably under cover (see pages 202–203 and 220).

DEFINE + REFINE

For the crisp look, choose materials such as stainless steel, aluminum, glass, plastics, laminates, and smooth wood with a subtle grain.

BARE NECESSITIES

Keep windows bare, if possible; but if the view, privacy, or keeping out the cold are issues, use blinds, shades, shutters, fabric panels, or simple, unfussy curtains.

COLOR INTENSITY

Control those colors, and restrict that palette. Avoid cheap-looking finishes and bright colors, and go for the sophisticated and subtle instead.

SEE THE LIGHT

Pay attention to the lighting. There are plenty of smart, simple, and surprisingly inexpensive light fixtures around—aluminum and frosted glass are perfect for the modern look.

3 **thrifty** shopping

shopaholics anonymous

Conspicuous consumption is so "last year," but thrifty people with shopaholic tendencies don't have to miss out on their favorite pastime. In fact, a nose for a bargain, an instinct for what's likely to be the next big trend, plus a willingness to spend hours in pursuit of the perfect purchase are great assets. Just make sure these are accompanied by self-control, a clear idea of what you are looking for, the ability to say no, and the patience to wait for what you really want.

canny shopping tips

There was a time when good design and fashionable style were available only at the high and expensive, end of the market. Today you can find both in a wide variety of places. Read on.

● CHAIN STORE SHOPPING

Every wise shopper who buys clothes from the large chain stores knows not to buy distinctive designs, in order to avoid advertising exactly where they shop and meeting others who are similarly dressed. Smart shoppers buy the basics and then dress them up to create a style that is their own. This applies equally to interiors, where canny customers buy chain store items that will be a discreet presence in the home rather than a bold statement.

●● SALE-TIME SHOPPING

If you have champagne taste but a mineral water budget, the sales are for you. Keep an eye on the smartest stores, and make sure you know when their sales are on. Join their mailing list, or check their web site regularly for special offers, reductions, stock clearances, or even closing-down sales. Most high-class stores have sale previews, so go along to see if it's worth packing the thermos and sandwiches ready to line up for a chance of getting your chosen bargain. Along with great sale reductions, the better stores often run a 10 percent or more discount offer on normal stock, which can make the previously unaffordable just about possible. Canny shoppers also visit sales in their late stages, when prices are further reduced. Anxious to get rid of stuff, stores offer better bargains and may even agree to haggle.

●● ART GALLERIES + MUSEUMS

If you're looking for a piece of art and can't trust your judgment, opt for good-quality reproductions of the finest world art from art galleries and museums. Grace a side table with a reproduction of a fabulous ancient sculpture or a wall with a stunning Klee, Kandinsky, or Picasso. Everyone will praise you for your great sense of style.

pay the price

Thrift isn't only about low prices. Buying cheap may solve any current budget deficiencies, but it could turn out to be a false economy.

SOFA SENSE

For example, it may seem sensible to buy an inexpensive sofa if it's going to be subjected to the ravages of children or pets; but a more expensive, good-quality sofa will be more durable and can be cleaned or re-covered as needed later on.

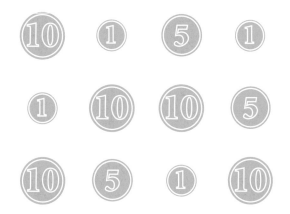

BEST INVEST

For the cost of several budget buys, invest in one beautiful piece that will last and may even appreciate in value. The difference in quality and/or style could be worth much more than the difference in price.

LASTING IMPRESSION

Fashions come and go, but classics stay the course. Spend money on quality items and on good but simple designs that are capable of living through the fads and fancies of one era to obligingly fit in with the next.

CORE COLLECTION

Remember that it's often better to blow a whole budget on one or two good pieces. They will be the center of attraction now and the core of a collection for the future.

MUST-HAVE CHOICE

Investing a little more in one item you adore is a more satisfying way of spending your money than buying lots of inexpensive things you don't love.

tempted?

There are so many well-designed, good-looking, inexpensive products on the market that it's easy to give in to the temptation to buy more than you really need. A visit to the out-of-town furniture store can soon develop into an orgy of buying; decisions on what to purchase are often clouded by the sheer cheapness of the items for sale. The result? A nasty shock at the checkout when you realize that, cheap though the individual items may be, buying a lot can prove expensive. Also, you'll find yourself with an unruly assemblage of small, disparate items in your home, rather than a considered, coherent collection.

To avoid inadvertent overspending, have a clear idea of what you need before you go shopping. Make a list and stick to it. If something is out of stock, don't rush into buying an alternative. It's better to place an order and wait for the item you really want than to settle for second best.

patience is a virtue

■ Take time to decide exactly what you want; and if it isn't available right away, be prepared to wait for it to turn up in a store, at a salesroom, or on the Internet.

■ Building a collection slowly over time lessens the likelihood of impulse buying.

■ Collecting things slowly over a number of years can be a positive experience. You'll be sure to appreciate every new, carefully chosen item a little more.

■ If in doubt, don't.

 thrifty shopping

DID YOU KNOW THAT...?

. . . one of the things that distinguish expensive furnishings from inexpensive is scale. Economy products are often made using less material. The result? Proportions are not as generous, and a budget buy can end up looking like the poor relation. Take a cheap sofa or chest, for example. It can look skimpy and insignificant and will detract from an otherwise attractive interior. The skimpiness applies not only to the item's height, width, and depth but also to the thickness of materials used—look for robust and chunky, rather than thin—and the size of detailing and fittings, such as knobs and handles.

tips for buying **cheap**

SOLID STUFF

Much of the cheapest furniture available is made from fiberboard finished with wood or plastic laminate. While it looks okay, the edges are prone to damage. Solid wood always looks and wears better and can be treated with paint, stain, or wax to improve its life expectancy or to give it a complete makeover.

COLOR CHIC

Inexpensive fabrics and laminates can look cheap in bright colors, so try to stick to whites and neutrals.

VARNISH VANDALISM

Soft woods are sometimes given a coating of varnish to make them more hard-wearing, but the result can look cheap and shoddy. Use paint or stain to cover such inadequacies.

cheapskate choice
1 **classics on the cheap**

The best modern design is elegant, seductive, perfectly formed, beautifully made, and usually very expensive. Original, classic modern designs come with scary price tags, but as long as you look after them they can increase in value, so they could be considered a good investment.

If only the best will do, the thrifty solution is to forego all vacations, evenings out, and having a fully furnished house in order to purchase that special something. Or, if you're clever and can spot an up-and-coming designer, scour student degree shows and exhibitions for the collectibles of the future. You could even commission a piece made to your specifications.

While investing in those genuine design classics may be out of your reach, there are plenty of good imitations around with the same clean lines and shapes. Mass production offers a high level of quality at surprisingly low prices.

STUDIO COUCH

Consisting of square-edged cushions on a metal frame, this type of sofa is usually inexpensive. It looks smarter than a futon and takes up less space. Leave it plain, or soften the effect with pillows and throws.

CAFÉ FURNITURE

Based on an original Spanish design, café chairs and tables can be seen in coffee shops the world over. Cheaper versions are now making their appearance in chain stores. Perfect for outdoors, they also look good in a modern kitchen.

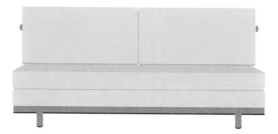

PLYWOOD FRAME ARMCHAIR

Reminiscent of the designs of Marcel Breuer and Bruno Mathsson, this chair (below, left) is a classic in its own right. Very comfortable, especially with a matching footstool.

PLYWOOD DINING CHAIR

The popularity and versatility of Arne Jacobsen's Series 7 stacking chairs have led to a number of imitations (below, right). Some are more blatant copies than others, but all possess an elegance and provide the opportunity for a splash of color in your room.

DESK LAMPS

The best of these echo the workmanlike shapes and proportions of the original Anglepoise desk lamp, designed in 1934 (below, left). The modern versions work well as table lamps, bedside lights, task lighting, and, with a special floor-standing pole, as floor lamps.

MODULAR UNITS

Some modular units are a variation on the simple cube storage systems of the early 1960s, while others are sophisticated designs that poach ideas from Jean Prouvé (below, right) and Charles and Ray Eames.

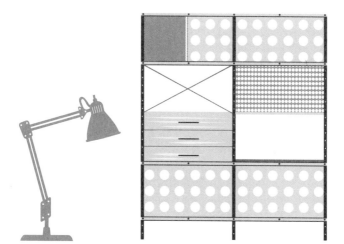

cheapskate choice
2 **low cost, high style**

CLIP-ON LAMPS

Sophisticated lighting systems are expensive, since they require a qualified electrician to install the wires and fixtures. Clip-on lamps are no trouble at all. They need only a nearby outlet and somewhere safe where they can be securely attached. Use as task lights over a work surface or desk or as display lighting aimed at a picture or object. Direct them toward the ceiling or wall to provide subtle background lighting.

DIVANS

A new, narrow divan can be picked up for a song in a bed store. It makes a great sofa, studio couch, and, when required, a spare bed. Don't just throw a bedspread over it though, or it will look boring. Instead, layer it with throws and load it with pillows. Alternatively, make a smart, tailored cover for it or a fun, frilly one. Another option is to put two divans together to make a swish-looking corner sofa— normally an expensive purchase. If you want your divan to function well as a sofa, invest in some good-quality cushions to prop against the wall.

WOODEN BOXES

Home centers and large furniture chains sell a good selection of low-cost, stout, wooden-lidded boxes ready for staining or painting. They are, of course, great for storage, but can also be attractive pieces of furniture in their own right. Think low tables, seats (with the help of a comfy cushion), or useful surfaces for anything from the TV to a collection of precious objects. Several boxes side by side along a wall are a cheap alternative to modular storage, with the advantage that you can choose the color and finish.

BOX CUSHIONS

Large, soft floor cushions are great for lolling around on, but they clutter up the space and are not much use for anything else. The newer box cushions are neater, smarter, and more versatile. Some are made of firm foam, while others are stuffed with feathers or are constructed like a mattress. Although these are more expensive, three of them will still cost a lot less than a good-quality stool, chair, or bed.

- Stack your cushions and add a matching tray top to transform them into an occasional table.

- Spread three along the floor, and you have a comfortable, instant guest bed.

PENDANT LAMPSHADES

With an opaque metal shade, light escapes only from below, forming a pool of directional light. Stainless steel looks cool and modern, but colored enamel lined with white can be perfect in a retro or more casual environment. Translucent glass lets light out of the sides, as well as from below, providing a more diffused light. Plain white-etched glass is discreet and suits any style. A single pendant lampshade hung low over a table in a sparsely furnished room is very chic and atmospheric.

MULTIPLE PENDANT LAMPSHADES

Some pendant lampshades are so inexpensive that you can buy three of them for less than the price of a single more expensive version. So why not hang three or more in a row above a dining table?

cheapskate choice
3 grab a bargain

Antiques are naturally expensive, while secondhand used to mean cheap. Then "retro" became big business. The plethora of TV programs that inflate the value of anything old, from a chair to a cookie jar, has also raised the stakes, so sellers are less likely to let things go for a song. Getting real bargains in the resale market is becoming more difficult; but a keen eye and the ability to see beyond any shortcomings can still bring rewards, as well as being good fun.

●●● DEALERS

Genuine antiques are very expensive, but prices often compare favorably with the high end of new and the rising cost of "retro." Cultivate friendships with local antique dealers, and they'll keep an eye open for items at good prices for you. Also use these dealers to learn what to look for. With their help, you might recognize a lucky bargain in a thrift shop or a rummage or garage sale.

●● ANTIQUE FAIRS + MARKETS

The swankier antique fairs are held in exhibition centers, hotels, and town halls, and often involve serious money. More modest affairs, held in streets, marketplaces, and church social halls, have lower prices. But even here, goods can range from genuine bargains to the scandalously overpriced, so do your research to get some idea of what to look for and what's a fair price.

●● SALESROOMS

Visit a few salesrooms before you buy to get some idea of prices; then, when you've found what you're looking for, examine it carefully before you bid, and decide if the item's what you want (could it be the next fashion?). Prices vary, depending on how trendy the item is and how many dealers are bidding. Remember, a dealer needs to sell his or her goods on at a much higher price, so a winning bid could still be below the market value.

If you're willing to pay a good price, make sure the item's in good condition. Paying full price for something you have to spend a lot of time and money on putting right is not thrift sense.

● FLEA MARKETS

The distinction between antique and flea markets is rather blurred, but flea markets are usually held outdoors. Small-town markets in less touristy or trendy areas are more likely to yield bargains than other places. Markets abroad offer a less familiar, and possibly more interesting, selection of goods.

●●● SALVAGE YARDS

Great places for finding old doors, window frames, floorboards, moldings, stone sinks, cast-iron bathtubs and many unusual items of architectural interest. They can be expensive, because this sort of stuff is in great demand, but it may be worth the expense if you want to replace original fittings in properties where sensitive restoration is a worthwhile investment.

● USED OFFICE EQUIPMENT SUPPLIERS

In addition to desks, chairs, and filing cabinets, used office equipment suppliers also sell tables and upholstered seating. Among the steel tubing and laminate (a good "modern" material), you may find solid wood or metal desks, wooden flat files and sometimes old filing systems and pigeonhole shelves, which make great storage. School chairs, lockers, and cupboards are other items that offer good-quality design at reasonable prices.

●● INTERNET SHOPPING

Shopping on the Internet isn't the same as poking around in dusty curiosity shops, but if you're after something special, you can search the whole world with your mouse. The Internet is also a useful place for checking the value of what you want to buy or sell. When shopping on the Internet, use only reputable sites, and exercise caution when paying online. For private sales or purchases from smaller shops, make contact by telephone and make sure you have all the seller's details before making a payment.

● SECONDHAND STORES

Poking around in a crowded secondhand store is, for many, one of life's great pleasures. Frequent visits are recommended to get the pick of any new stock. Look for smaller items from estate sales, such as sets of tablelinen and china. Prices vary, but these are the sort of places where you can make an offer.

● THRIFT SHOPS

Plenty of bargains are to be had in thrift shops. The more enterprising ones rotate their stock, offering further reductions on items that don't sell quickly, to make space for new ones; patience could bring you extra rewards.

● GARAGE + YARD SALES

Finding something you want and need at an individual's garage or yard sale is a lucky accident; so go for community-wide sales. However, you need to get there early—knowledgable antique dealers and collectors are likely to arrive before you and snap up the best bargains.

● RUMMAGE SALES

You stand a good chance of bagging a bargain at a rummage sale, because the stuff isn't sorted beforehand and the people in charge aren't always tuned in to the latest design trends. The best buys are to be found in affluent areas, where the castoffs are likely to be of good quality.

● CLASSIFIED ADS
Fun to read, and you never know what might turn up.

○ DUMPSTERS
There are still exciting things lurking in dumpsters, but you have to get there first and be brazen enough to pillage in full view of passersby. Chippendale chairs are a rare find, but furniture from the 1960s and 1970s isn't. Perfectly good rugs are often chucked out, and it's worth looking in plastic bags for curtains and other textiles. Office furniture is another frequent find.

● SWAP SHOP
The ultimate in thrift is either buying from one of the growing number of furniture exchanges or swapping with friends and family. Older people are often willing to swap or give away furniture or textiles they think are outdated but that you know are trendy.

cheapskate choice
4 **cut-price prizes**

LAMPS

Lamps are simple to update with a fashionable new shade, but some styles can also look good with just a plain lightbulb. And watch for tall floor lamps, which are making a comeback.

BED FRAMES

Proper bed frames, especially wooden ones, are back in fashion. If the supporting base is missing, it's not too difficult to make a new slatted one from scraps of lumber.

COATRACKS

These add character to any hallway, as well as keeping coats, hats, and umbrellas under control. Occasionally you'll find solid oak coatracks, but most often they're dark wood, which could look better painted. Some have a mirror.

ARMCHAIRS WITH WOODEN ARMS

There's a plentiful supply of armchairs with wooden arms. They are neither as big nor as expensive as a fully upholstered chair, and so are good for small spaces. They are also easier and cheaper to freshen up with a tie-on chair cover.

RUGS + MATS

Old rugs and mats can often be bought at giveaway prices. Threadbare can be chic, but grubby isn't, in which case get to work with some carpet shampoo. Try several rugs in layers, with the not-so-attractive specimens at the bottom.

SMALL CABINETS + UNITS

You're bound to find a use for a pretty little cabinet or shelf, whether it's delightfully dilapidated or needs to be freshened up with a new coat of paint. If you find any old wall units, hang them in twos and threes— they definitely don't have to match.

WALLPAPER

Wallcoverings are back—and the older, the better. Wallpaper that you would have taken the stripper to only a few years ago suddenly looks desirable.

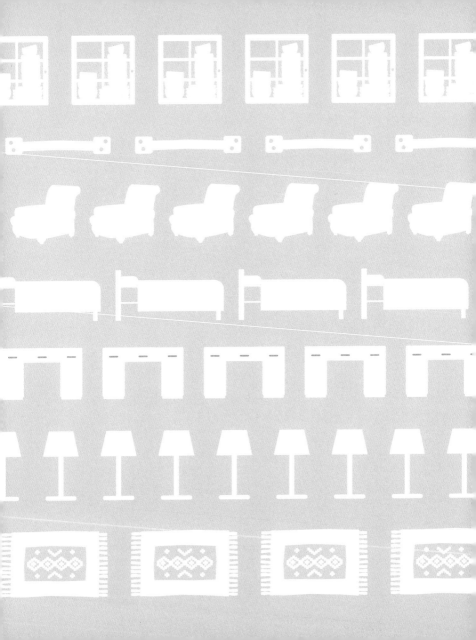

DOORKNOBS + HANDLES

It's not essential to have matching doorknobs or handles throughout your house, or even on a single piece of furniture. If you find something special, put it to good use.

ODD TILES

If you like the cozy, casual look and are feeling creative, a patchwork of odd tiles in your kitchen or bathroom can look great.

WRITING DESKS

An old-fashioned writing desk is an incredibly useful piece of furniture for keeping all your paperwork. A fall front provides space for a laptop computer or for writing good old-fashioned letters. Look beyond first impressions; if the finish isn't very appealing, give it a coat of paint or stain.

PICTURE FRAMES + MIRRORS

There are still bargains to be had. Look especially for large, fancy picture frames, and smarten them up or tone them down with paint. Seek out those old, interestingly shaped mirrors that our grandparents used to hang by a chain above the living room mantelpiece. They are equally at home in a bedroom or bathroom. For fun, hang them in twos and threes.

LINENS

Old cotton and linen is often thicker and softer than its new equivalent, and prices can still be surprisingly low. In addition to sheets and pillowcases, look for tablecloths, runners, napkins, and good, old-fashioned antimacassars, especially if they are hand embroidered or edged in lace.

BLANKETS, RUGS + THROWS

With duvets becoming increasingly popular, there are plenty of blankets lurking in junk shops, rummage sales, and thrift shops. Pick out clean, good-quality woolen blankets and give them a good wash. You may be lucky and find old ones with fashionable stripes or windowpane plaids, but traditional cream or even pink blankets can look very good. And don't forget to take a second look at those candlewick bedspreads.

KITCHEN EQUIPMENT

Keep an eye open for old canisters, utensils, pots and pans, bread bins and breadboards, cake tins, and silverware.

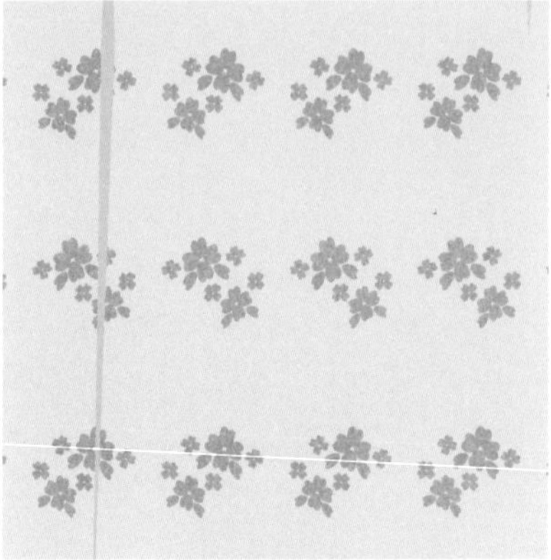
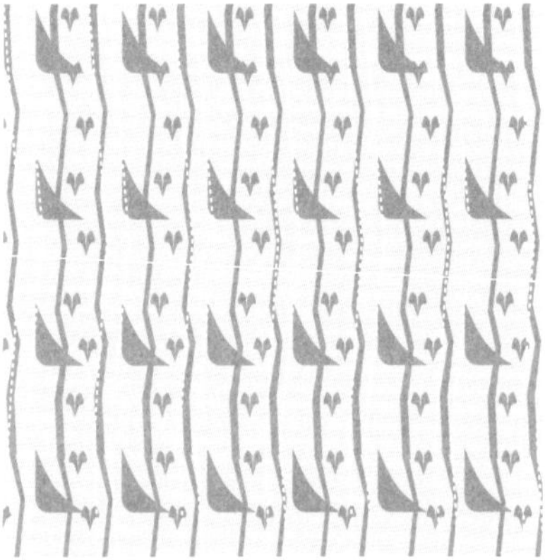
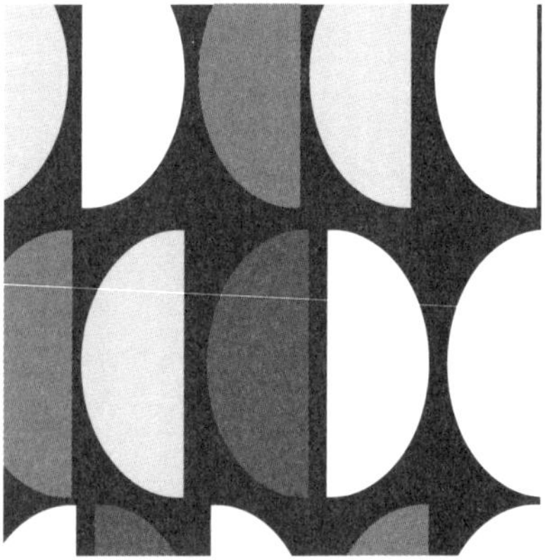
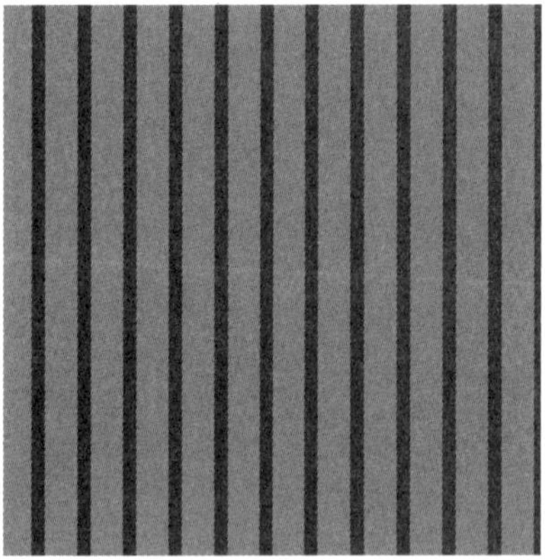
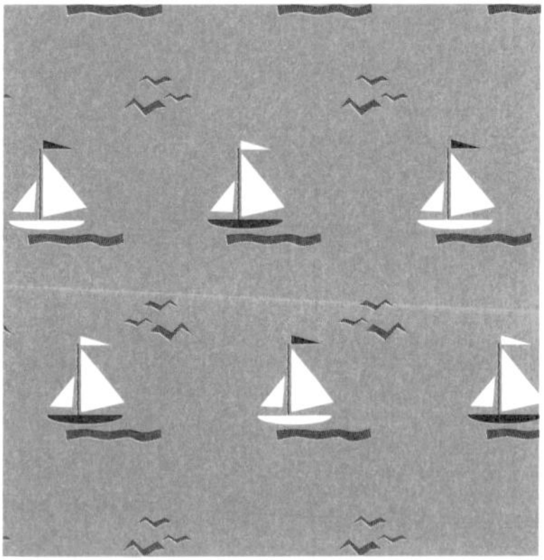

cheapskate choice
5 **fabric shopping**

COTTONS

Inexpensive cottons—including dress fabrics, which are cheaper than furnishing fabrics and make perfect, simple curtains—can be picked up in markets and shops in less affluent areas. In addition to pretty prints, there are stripes, dots, and ginghams. Thrifty travelers will pick up Provençal prints in the south of France and colorful cottons in Central and South America, Asia, and Africa. Otherwise find them in your local ethnic shops and flea markets.

UTILITARIAN FABRICS

These are inexpensive, and their simplicity makes them appealing. Unbleached muslin is great, but it shrinks, so wash it before sewing. Ticking has a pleasing crisp appearance, is hard-wearing, and is available in a variety of stripes. Denim not only is hard-wearing but famously improves with age. And, just as jeans go with anything from a crisp white shirt to a sexy, silky top, so denim looks comfortable in many styles of decor.

BED LINENS

If you particularly like the color and design of a duvet cover, you could cut it up and turn it into curtains and covers. Otherwise, use inexpensive flat bed sheets, which give you a lot of fabric for your money. They're wider than fabric bought by the yard, and they come already edged (though you could unpick the stitching along the sides of the top hem and thread them onto a rod to make an unusual curtain). Pure cotton is best; synthetics look too much like the sheets they really are, which is not a desirable effect.

OLD + BOLD

Thrift shops and secondhand stores are a good source of seemingly outdated designs that only you and others in the know realize are the latest thing. Bold fabrics from the 1960s and 1970s, which until even fairly recently wouldn't have been given houseroom, suddenly look absolutely perfect for brightening up a sterile modern space.

REMNANTS + SCRAPS

Dive into the remnant table in furnishing and dress fabric departments for the opportunity to buy a piece of fabric that would otherwise be way beyond your means. A small length of a very special fabric made into a pillow cover or chair cover or used for some patchwork or appliqué will inject a dash of magic in your room.

outdoors indoors

Thrifty furniture sometimes requires a little alternative thinking. Scour the home centers and garden centers for garden furniture that you could adapt for indoor use.

● GARDEN BENCH

Plain wooden garden benches can become indoor seating with a coat of paint and some seat cushions. Besides looking good, extra cushions or draped throws and quilts provide added comfort. Perfect for a summery, seaside feel and great in your kitchen.

● PICNIC TABLE + BENCHES

Extremely good value for very little money, a picnic table with benches can be painted in thick gloss paint and used in a kitchen dinette. For extra comfort, add cushions. Be warned though: these picnic benches are quite wide so they may not suit a cramped space.

DID YOU KNOW THAT...?

... according to eBay, dealers and collectors tend to use the term "antique" to describe something that is at least 100 years old. "Collectibles" are generally about 25 to 100 years old, and "vintage" is a catchall word that means "not brand-new." Sellers often describe an item as "vintage" if they don't know how old the item is, but know it was made at least a decade ago.

old styles to shop for

Encouraged by TV programs that reveal the potential value of our possessions, far more people are now in the know about the price of old things. This makes for higher prices, which is bad news for people on low budgets. But sometimes it is sound thrift sense to invest in good-quality pieces that will last for many years and appreciate in value. Here is a brief roundup of popular styles that may do just that.

late **georgian**

The elegance of Georgian architecture—also known, in the United States, as "colonial"— has inspired the interior fashion for paneled walls and doors, bare floorboards, and woodwork painted in muted greens. Favored furniture includes deep armchairs, chaises longues, and curvy-legged tables, just like those used by the upstairs aristocracy. But even more in demand is the stuff used by those below stairs, such as metal bed frames, large, solid armoires, and plain wooden chairs and tables, as well as all manner of kitchen paraphernalia, from stone sinks to oversized ceramic bowls and pitchers. Original wooden paneling, floorboards, sinks, basins, and other sanitary ware can be found in salvage yards, but expect to pay the going price.

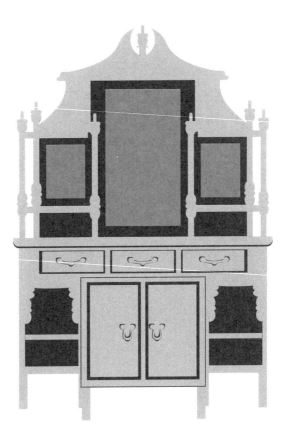

victoriana **style**

Not so long ago, heavy, highly carved—and curved—Victorian furniture enjoyed a brief vogue among young people setting up house for the first time, and this drove prices up. More recently, however, the fashion for minimalist interiors has lessened its appeal, so it should be possible to find a few bargains in the form of dining tables and chairs, large chiffoniers, armchairs, and sofas. Also look for small delicate tables, cake stands, trays, odd bits of china, cutlery, cruet sets, and pieces of silver.

arts and crafts
+ mission style

William Morris was the prime mover of this nineteenth-century movement, the ideals of which centered on quality materials and craftsmanship. In the United States, the same principles informed the later Mission furniture of Gustave Stickley and others. Morris advised people to "have nothing in your houses that you do not know to be useful, or believe to be beautiful." Arts and Crafts furniture ranges from solid-looking cupboards, cabinets, and settles to more delicate, rush-seated chairs. Many of the original pieces were painted in dark colors and decorated with images. Because they were handcrafted, rather than mass produced, examples by original members of the Arts and Crafts movement will be very expensive. However, the term is often applied to craftsman-made, simple, solid furniture from around the beginning of the twentieth century, the price of which represents good value, compared to new pieces of similar quality.

twentieth-century **modern**

This term is used to describe a wide range of modernist furniture, from the design classics of the Bauhaus era to the more recent designs of the 1960s and 1970s. Much of the furniture from these later periods has just been rediscovered, and pieces that were destined for dumpsters a few years ago are now demanding eyebrow-raising prices. Unless in very poor condition, vintage pieces by Marcel Breuer, Le Corbusier, Eero Saarinen, and Charles and Ray Eames will be very pricey, as will originals by Scandinavian designers such as Alvar Aalto, Arne Jacobsen, and Hans Wegner. Items by the British husband-and-wife design team Robin and Lucienne Day are also keenly collected. Some design classics are still being produced (at commensurately steep prices) by leading furniture manufacturers. There are also lots of copies, of varying quality. Knowing your styles and designers is essential, so you'll need to do some research before you buy. If you can't afford some of the bigger pieces, console yourself with items such as ceramics, glassware, and textiles.

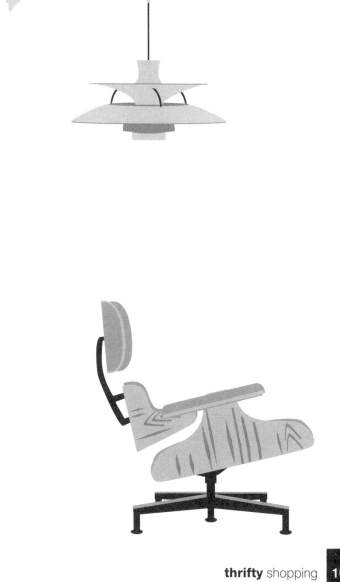

shaker style

In recent years, Shaker-style furniture has become immensely popular. The Shakers were an English religious sect (now almost extinct) who settled in the American Colonies in the eighteenth century. Their way of life was characterized by extreme simplicity, and so was the furniture they created. Authentic Shaker antiques fetch huge prices, but you can find high-quality reproductions by modern cabinetmakers, ranging from bureaus and ladder-back chairs down to hatboxes and wastebaskets. Even mass-produced Shaker-style furniture is worth investigating; but first do a little research to become familiar with the real thing so that you can shop with an informed eye. Shaker-inspired kitchen and bathroom cabinets are also available.

retro + nostalgia

There's a crossover with twentieth-century modern, but "retro" (from "retrospective") usually applies to any pieces that are reminiscent of the 1940s and 1950s diner look, with lots of chrome, leather, plastic, and bright colors. As the "diner" image suggests, retro is most at home in the kitchen. Such items as dinette sets with booth seats, barstools with tubular steel legs, and Formica countertops are "classic" retro. Tableware in primary colors, chunky ice-cream soda glasses, and bright floral-printed curtains enhance the effect. In other rooms, go for the quirky, from the 1950s and later—beanbag chairs and lava lamps, for example—and set it all off with gloss paint or big abstract-print wallpaper.

a word of **caution**

ELECTRICAL GOODS

Old electric heaters are potentially dangerous, so unless you know your way around electricity, you should leave them alone. Your insurance company may refuse to pay up if they suspect a fire was caused by dubious equipment sold through a nonregulated outlet. As with lighting (see opposite), check all cables and connections. Don't forget that foreign appliances are likely to be incompatible.

WOODWORM

Check any wooden items for signs of live woodworm; fresh holes and deposits of sawdust are a reliable indication. It's relatively easy to treat a small item using a proprietory product, which can be either brushed on or squirted into the holes with a syringe. It's wise to treat any infested items before you bring them into your home; that way, you won't allow the woodworm the run of the rest of your house.

LIGHTING
There's still lots of old bargain lighting to be had. Look for desk lamps, lamp bases, and shades from the 1930s and 1940s. Center light fixtures, often featuring colored or patterned glass, were popular from the 1950s to the 1970s; once much reviled, they are now very fashionable. Chandeliers are also back in favor and odd, pretty glass lampshades can still be quite cheap. Check all plugs, cables, and cords, and replace if they look at all unsafe.

COOKING RANGES

A vintage range may complement your kitchen perfectly, but it has to comply with the rules regarding safety. Any secondhand gas range sold by a retailer is required by law to have undergone a series of safety checks. And all ranges, whether bought from a store or privately, must be installed by a licensed contractor, who will carry out the appropriate safety checks.

RADIATORS

Cast-iron column radiators look great in old and modern homes alike. The real thing can be found in salvage yards and on the Internet. But though they look great, these radiators often aren't terribly efficient, so get an expert to give them the once-over. If your pipework is a different size, this could make installing old radiators complicated. A new copy might be a better thrifty purchase.

4 **thrifty** recycling

make do + amend
1 get out the china

○ FORMAL DINING
Dinner services and tea sets evoke a more formal yet leisurely approach to dining. For thrifty people, for whom eating in is the new eating out, formal dining and afternoon tea are not only great antidotes to fast food and fast living but also an opportunity to appreciate good food and get out Grandma's china.

● PLAIN + FANCY
Brighten up plain new dishes by mixing in a few pretty floral pieces that are lurking unused in the back of your cabinets.

 **114** **thrifty** recycling

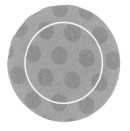

**"make do +
amend" means**
not going shopping,
but making the most
of what you've
already got.

make do + amend
2 **all lit up**

● **LAMP BASES**

Modern lighting design is sleek and functional, and much of it is very inexpensive. But don't dismiss old lamp bases or floor lamps, for they can be given a new lease on life with a plain drum shade. Some even look all right with just a bare bulb, especially as there are lots of new shapes to choose from.

○ **LAMPSHADES**

Old-fashioned shades look quirky and friendly, so why not hang on to them and maybe team them with a modern lamp base?

make do + amend
3 **dining furniture**

●● SUITES

Dining suites are sometimes thrown out, because they're considered old-fashioned, but give them a second chance. A good-sized table and set of chairs in a kitchen or living room may inspire "proper" family meal times, and one of the best ways of entertaining friends is around a table laden with good food and wine. A dining table can also be the place for homework, sewing, and other mundane pursuits.

●● SIDEBOARDS

Sideboards are incredibly useful and are back in favor. Traditionally providing a home for table linen, drinks, and glasses, they still perform that function very well but are also good for CDs, DVDs, and even sound systems. Learn to appreciate the solid wood sideboards of the 1930s and 1940s, the lighter, more idiosyncratic shapes of the 1950s, and the long, low styles from the 1960s and 1970s.

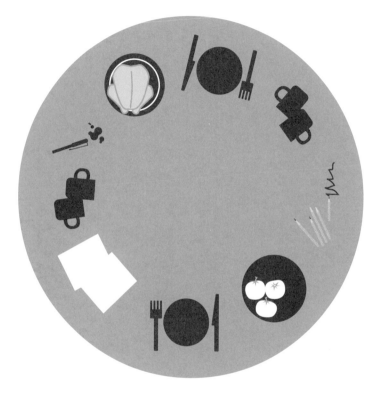

make do + amend
4 **dressing tables**

● The humble dressing table, once deemed old-fashioned and outmoded, was discarded in favor of vanity cabinets. But recently it has been sneaking back into fashion, along with the penchant for glamour and dressing up. Reconfigure and rejuvenate an old dressing table with a fresh coat of paint in a brilliant, unexpected color. If necessary, remove damaged or ugly mirrors, moldings, and knobs and handles, and replace them with new or funky alternatives.

make do + amend
5 **drawers + dressers**

● If you've got your clothes storage sorted out and find you have a spare chest of drawers, it could be given a new lease on life in the kitchen. The drawers of a chest can be used for anything from table linen to packages of rice. Hang an inexpensive shelf unit above it, paint them both the same color, and you have an instant kitchen dresser—a place to store and show off your best china.

thrifty recycling

don't make over—**clean**

When a home's looking tired and scruffy, it's too easy to think that nothing short of a complete makeover will bring it back to life. We all know how a room responds to a quick tidy and a bit of fresh air, so think what a thorough wash and brushup could do. This is not only cheap but thrifty, too, as it will ensure that your furniture and furnishings last longer.

use a **pro**

Cleaning has been described as "the new sex." This may be stretching a point, but there's no doubt that good housekeeping has gained a higher profile in recent years. But if cleaning really isn't your thing, consider getting in a professional company to do the job for you. Obviously it will cost more, but it can be the thrifty option, especially if you have valuable furniture and furnishings or high-quality flooring that needs careful treatment.

cleaning tips

WHERE DO I START?

The place to begin is at the top of the house or at the back of the apartment so you're not passing through already-cleaned areas to get to the unclean. And start at the top of each room—ceilings first, floors last.

BUST THE DUST

Dust turns to dirt when it comes into contact with water, so removing it from every surface first (a vacuum cleaner is good for this) makes sense, particularly on surfaces that are to be washed down.

WALL WIZARDRY

It's not necessary to wash walls, but obvious dirt and stains around light switches or in areas of heavy traffic can be removed with mild detergent. However, you might end up with a spanking-clean patch, so it may be best to wash the whole wall or repaint.

GENTLY DOES IT

Wash splashes and scuffs from woodwork using a soft scouring sponge, but don't scrub too hard, or you'll abrade the surface and more dirt will cling.

HARD FLOORS . . .

thrifty recycling

Rewax or re-oil a wooden floor as needed, and wash a varnished floor with a damp mop; apply more varnish if the surface is worn. Mop a painted floor using mild detergent, and repaint or reseal if required. Use soap, rather than detergent, to wash stone floors. Ceramic tiles and vinyl benefit from a good scrub.

. . . AND SOFT ONES

Vacuum carpets thoroughly, and shampoo only if necessary; shampooing too frequently destroys the carpet's natural stain-retardant properties.

FAB FABRICS

It isn't necessary to dry-clean heavy draperies or slipcovers every year, so if they've recently been cleaned, just give them a good vacuuming.

BLINDS AND SHADES

Wash, dry-clean, or vacuum Roman shades. Wash plastic or metal venetian blinds in the bathtub or under the shower using mild detergent. Wooden venetian blinds should be dusted or wiped with a damp cloth in situ.

5 **thrifty** home improvements

a lick of **paint**

Sometimes a cheering coat of paint is all a home needs. Paint is eminently affordable, so miracles can be achieved for a surprisingly thrifty sum.

PLAIN HOUSE PAINTOVER
The shortcomings of a plain or relatively characterless house will be less obvious with careful use of paint. Use the same color for walls and woodwork, and unattractive features will blend into the background.

DAMAGED HOUSE PAINTOVER
Rough, damaged, or patchy surfaces can be painted over, and you'll find that imperfections become virtually invisible, especially once your possessions are in place.

LOVELY HOUSE PAINTOVER

In a characterful and architecturally beautiful home, a coat of paint will emphasize the good points and pleasing proportions and will allow any distinguishing features to take center stage. Pick out quality woodwork using glamorous glossy or muted matte paint in harmonizing or contrasting colors.

WHOLE HOUSE PAINTOVER

Any house can look bright, clean, and beautiful after a liberal application of white or very pale paint. The added bonus is that it will look and feel bigger, which is particularly good for small houses or rooms.

DIY decorator

■ Walls and ceilings that are in good condition require only a quick dusting down. If they're very dirty or covered in remnants of wallpaper, they should be washed with a warm, mild solution of detergent, followed by plain water. Any paper should then be removed.

■ Woodwork should be rubbed down using abrasive paper or washed with de-greaser to provide a "tooth" for the new coat of paint.

■ Untreated wood and metal need primer to protect them and provide a good base for the paint. You can now buy primers for shiny surfaces, such as melamine, kitchen cabinets, tiles, and other items with a shiny finish.

PAINT . . .

■ Buy paints made by one of the large manufacturers, as they're often cheaper than specialist paints and come in a huge range of colors. Normally, latex flat is used on walls, gloss or eggshell on woodwork. Modern washable latex flat can also be used on woodwork that isn't exposed to heavy wear.

■ Traditionally, gloss and eggshell paints have been oil based, which made them smelly and a potential health hazard. These paints are now being phased out, and water-based, low-VOC (Volatile Organic Compound) versions are being introduced. They are more pleasant to use and dry much quicker.

■ There's no doubt that some specialist paint ranges include the most wonderful colors and give a distinctly different finish. If paint is your passion, it may well be worth the extra expense. Architecturally beautiful houses should always be treated with respect. Besides being historically correct, some of these paints will enhance such a building's appearance.

thrifty home improvements

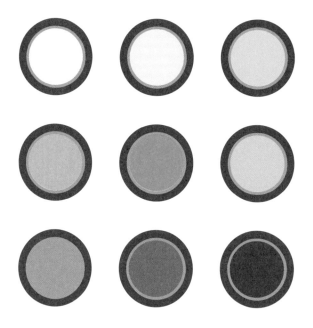

DON'T PAINT . . .

You can save money and effort by leaving woodwork unpainted. Some evidence of age, such as chips and flakes, can be attractive, but dirty and damaged paintwork is not, so get cleaning (see pages 122–125).

what **lurks** underneath?

Removing the dirt (see pages 122–125), dreadful decoration, and damaged or unnecessary fixtures and fittings from your home is a great way to reveal its good points. You may even be pleasantly surprised to discover that a relatively inexpensive program of repairs and some rearranging of the space will produce the home you've always wanted and didn't know you had.

DID YOU KNOW THAT...?

. . . new moldings and baseboards will pull a room together and don't cost very much. For a crisp, clean look use square-edged lengths of wood. For greater definition, make them deep and chunky.

increase the sense of space
1 **clever color scheming**

● One of the most effective ways of making your home feel light and spacious is to restrict yourself to one floor finish and one wall color and use these throughout. That way, the rooms will appear to flow into one another.

thrifty home improvements

increase the sense of space
2 removing/opening doors

O Simply removing the doors between the kitchen, hall, and living areas will create the illusion of one big space. But if this is likely to cause an unacceptable level of noise or a problem with cooking smells, think carefully before you do it. The less drastic alternative of just propping doors open will also create an impression of more space, particularly if you continue the same decorative scheme throughout all the rooms (see oppposite).

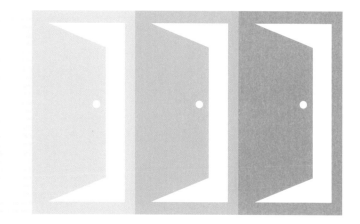

increase the sense of space
3 **door + window changes**

● SOLID TO SEE-THROUGH

A cheaper alternative to removing walls to achieve a large, light-filled space is to replace solid doors with glass-paneled ones. These are readily available at home centers and are relatively inexpensive.

●● WINDOW TO DOOR

Replacing a window with glass-paneled French doors is not too much trouble and will make a room not only lighter but more elegant.

●●● WALL TO WINDOW

For a dramatic effect, replace a whole wall with large patio doors. This will be expensive, since it entails putting in supporting beams and employing experts, but it's not hugely expensive for the impact it will make.

thrifty home improvements

increase the
sense of space
4 improve
the lighting
When it comes to lighting,
limited resources do not mean
limited options. Lighting comes
in a huge range of choices, and
much of it is remarkably
inexpensive.

●● SPOTLIGHTS + DOWNLIGHTERS

These give overall illumination. Styles vary from standard spotlights, available singly or in rows or groups, to lights on adventurous, curved metal frames. Recessed downlighters are popular for living areas and kitchens. They look modern and give an overall wash of light, but they don't suit all ceilings and should be professionally installed.

●● CENTER LIGHTS

The interest in retro has led to a reappraisal of the lone central ceiling light. Drum shades made of fabric, paper shades, glass shades—whether clear or frosted—and chandeliers are all back in favor.

●● PENDANT LIGHTS

A long cord on a ceiling light turns it into a pendant. A paper lantern hung low in a corner looks effective. Rows of pendant lights are trendy and are a good alternative to spotlights or downlighters for a kitchen work surface or dining table.

●● WALL LIGHTS

Much subtler than overhead lighting. Some require wiring into the wall, which can be an expensive bother, but there are plug-in versions, too. Single, plug-in spotlights fixed in a row halfway up the wall are cheap and easy to install and can be angled to create a variety of effects.

● TASK LIGHTING

Desk lamps provide good illumination for reading, knitting, and even cooking, but they can also be angled to give general light. Floor lamps can be placed next to a chair or desk, where they double as spotlights. Keep an eye out for older versions (see page 71) and for new, cheap and stylish aluminum photographers' lamps.

● LAMP BASES

Slim metal lamp bases complement most interior styles, but ceramic bases are back in fashion and come in all guises, from fancy urn shapes to simple designs finished with plain matte glazes. Old, turned wooden lamp bases often turn up in junk shops; they can be stripped and polished or painted and used either with a modern, plain drum shade or with a pretty, patterned shade for a nostalgic effect.

thrifty home improvements

• DISPLAY LIGHTING

Plug-in downlighters with their own transformers can be fixed underneath shelves and inside cabinets to highlight your possessions. Picture lights were once considered pretentious, but if you've got a stunning picture, why not make the most of it?

• FEATURE LIGHTS

Christmas lights, or versions of them, are easy to plug in and provide limitless possibilities. String them along shelves, behind beds or across walls.

• MAKE YOUR OWN

Make your own lamps using lamp kits available from home centers and crafts supplies stores. Be daringly kitsch and attach the fitting to a Chianti bottle, or be terribly arty and attach it to a narrow-necked vase filled with pebbles or marbles.

• LOOP THE LOOP

To save the expense of moving a light fixture, use a long cord looped through a hook screwed into the ceiling, and hang the light wherever you want it.

increase the sense of space
5 **rethink your space**

●● If moving home or getting in an architect simply isn't a viable option, it's possible to achieve amazing results just by changing how you allocate your space.

UPSTAIRS

Consider turning your house upside down, by moving living areas upstairs and bedrooms downstairs. This makes the most of the upstairs views and daylight.

If you crave privacy, a small, seldom-used storage room could double as a private retreat.

A generous bedroom could provide a sitting area that's out of bounds to the rest of the household.

DOWNSTAIRS

Make the most of any nooks and crannies, especially the space under the stairs. This could successfully be made into a closet, powder room, or shower room. Or you could open it up and remodel as a work area, or use the space for extra seating-cum-spare bed.

DID YOU KNOW THAT...?

. . . people on a tight budget often dismiss thoughts of building work, fearing that it will be super-expensive. However, small-scale works cost hundreds, rather than thousands, and can make a big impact.

EXPENSIVE

- Major building works need the services of an architect, building inspector, structural engineer, and good contractors, none of whom come cheap.

- Electric wiring must be tackled by professionals, and plumbing is best done professionally, too. These heavy-duty jobs involve pulling up floors and knocking holes in walls.

- New floors may cause considerable disruption

when laid, but a professional job can produce a dramatic effect and be well worth the expense.

NOT AS EXPENSIVE AS YOU THINK

■ Plastering and skimming should definitely be done by an expert. Although they make a mess, they don't take long. Smooth walls and ceilings make a huge difference to the quality of a decorative scheme.

■ Small building works, such as taking down an interior wall or building a new one, are relatively easy and surprisingly inexpensive.

FREE

■ Sometimes all you need is your own labor and that of friends and family, plus a dose of enthusiasm and imagination.

thrifty home improvements

building checklist

Armed with a clipboard, go around your home and assess its condition. Note anything that needs attention, repair, removal, or reappraisal. Poke into every corner—including the roof space, if possible—and under flooring and wallcoverings to examine the state of walls, ceilings, floors, windows, doors, fixtures and fittings.

STRUCTURE

Is your home structurally sound? If necessary, hire someone to check for dry and wet rot and woodworm. Telltale signs are rotten wood, damp patches, mold, and funny smells. Damage isn't always obvious, so have a good look around; and if you have access to the roof space, check beams and roof timbers, and look for evidence of leaks.

FLOORS

Take up flooring to inspect the floors. You never know, you may find wonderful wood, beautiful tiles, or trendy linoleum gasping for air. Is there any damp? Are the floorboards good enough to strip, or are they better covered up? Can old parquet floors be revived?

If you have a solid floor, is the subfloor okay? Can tiles

be repaired or replaced? Can holes be filled, or is more drastic treatment required?

WALLS + CEILINGS

Tap walls and ceilings to check for holes and hidden damage. Is the surface in good condition? If not, can it be put right with filler, or does it need replastering? Does wallpaper need removing, or can it be painted or papered over?

WOODWORK

Check door frames, picture rails, moldings, and baseboards. Do they need rubbing down or stripping? If they are in poor condition, will a coat of paint suffice? Can they be repaired, or would it simply be easier to remove and replace them?

FIXTURES + FITTINGS

If they're badly made, too far gone to repair, or just plain ugly, strip out fixtures and fittings, including built-in cabinets and shelves.

WINDOWS

Do they fit? Are they in good condition? Do they need replacing, or will minor repairs, plus a good rubdown, a coat of paint, and new hardware do? Are they secure? Time to replace with patio doors or French doors?

DOORS

Do they fit and open and close properly? Do they need replacing? Do they need to be there? Would they be better hung the other way around? Would glass bring in more light? How are you going to treat them—strip, rub down, paint?

WIRING

Is the wiring safe? Do you have the latest fuse box? Do you know your circuits? Do you want to put in track lighting (in which case you'll need a new circuit) or new wiring for sound or communication systems? Do you want to reroute wiring and cables so they're safer and/or out of sight?

PLUMBING

Locate the main shutoff valve, and make sure you know where the pipes are. Do you want to relocate any part of the plumbing or the drainage?

GAS

Never touch anything to do with gas yourself, and get all gas appliances checked regularly by a registered expert. Does the furnace need updating? A new model will save you money and be more eco-friendly (see page 297). Do you have proper ventilation for gas appliances? Get an expert to check.

HEATING

Inspect your heating system for faults or leaks. Do you want to add or move registers or radiators? Do you want to add thermostats to existing registers or radiators? Do you want to install a new type of heating?

ENERGY ECO-CHECK

Have you had a home energy check? If not, get one. This will show you where you might be able to make improvements. For example, it will check if your insulation is in good order.

SMOKING NOT ALLOWED

Do you have a smoke alarm? If not, buy one now. They're cheap and easy to install.

increase the space
1 **knock down a wall**

●● While the thrifty approach may preclude major building works, knocking down one wall is relatively easy and not very expensive. Most people knocking down a wall opt to increase the size of a kitchen or living area by knocking through into an adjacent room. Sometimes this enables them to provide a great room, large area for cooking, dining, and relaxing.

Alternatively, you could consider knocking through into a hallway—a space that's often underused and that may have windows that would bring extra light into other rooms. Doing this, however, can mean opening the hall onto the stairs and bedrooms, so before you act, consider carefully whether knocking through may result in problem noise or smells.

Knocking through into a hallway works particularly well if you have an entrance porch. If you don't, then make provision for draftproofing the front door.

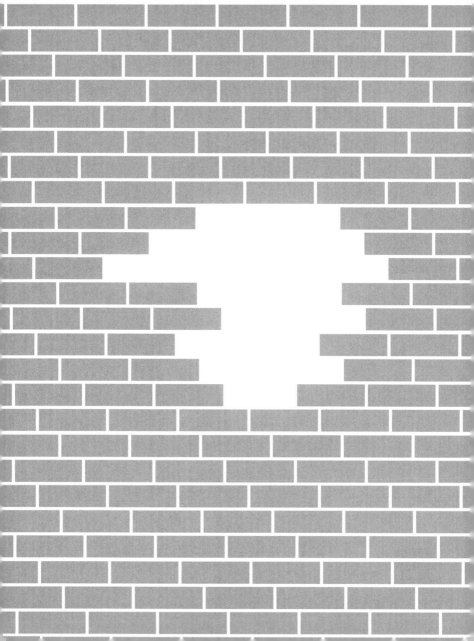

increase the space
2 **attic conversions**

●●● Attic conversions can be a lot cheaper than moving and can add value to your home. But they're not a cheap option and need to be done by a professional who'll make sure the work's carried out properly and complies with building codes. If you live in a townhouse or duplex house, don't forget to consult your neighbors; you may need permission from them to carry out any work on party walls. And before you get too excited, make sure there's room for a proper staircase—pull-down stairs are okay for infrequent use but not for every day. For attic rooms with sloping ceilings, a dormer window can increase the usable space; but be aware of your local building codes, and think carefully how the window will appear from the outside. A badly designed scheme not only will look horrible but could seriously damage the value of your home.

increase the space
3 **sheds + greenhouses**

● GET A SHED

Garden sheds don't have to be just for garden equipment. If you've really run out of room indoors but have spare space outdoors, add a shed. A small shed can take the pressure off indoor storage, and even a modest-sized version can act as a summerhouse, playhouse, studio, office, or refuge.

● LEAN AND LOVELY

If you can't afford a sunroom, consider a lean-to greenhouse. They're often reasonably priced, and there's no law saying you have to use them exclusively for plants.

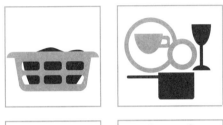

6 **thrifty** kitchens + bathrooms

priorities for **serious** cooks

If the kitchen really is the heart of your home, be prepared to lavish most of your budget on this one room. Spend wisely, take your time, do your research, and make sure you get good advice.

- If you do a lot of cooking, you should put an oven, work surfaces, and storage at the top of your priority list.

- Big ranges are great for serious cooks. Invest in the best you can afford.

- If you do tear out your old kitchen, avoid replacing it with a cheap option, for generally they aren't terribly robust. Go for cabinets in solid wood or high-quality laminate, and make sure they have good carcasses, hinges, runners, doors, and drawer fittings.

- A huge side-by-side refrigerator is extravagant if you use it only for pre-packaged meals, but if it's crammed with ingredients for top-quality meals, you'll get your money's worth.

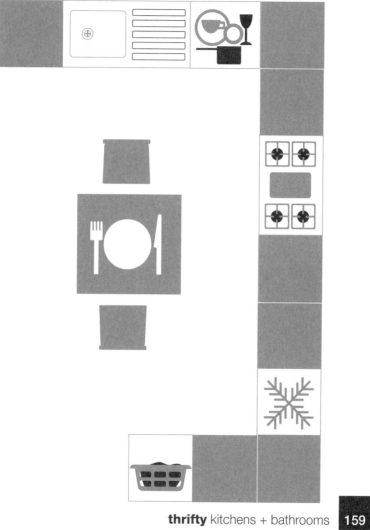

kitchens for **non-cooks**

If you're a busy person with no interest in cooking, who seldom entertains at home and uses the kitchen only for hot drinks and serving up takeouts, then inexpensive cabinets will suffice, since they won't be subjected to intense wear and tear. Go for a small, galley-style kitchen or a minimalist kitchen housed along one wall. That way, you can free up space for things that are more important to you.

But remember, lifestyles and circumstances change, so if you think there's a chance you will want to spend more time in the kitchen in the future, invest in altogether more hard-wearing and hardworking fixtures (see page 158).

DID YOU KNOW THAT...?

. . . there are lots of rules on kitchen layouts involving work triangles and what to put where, but rooms and lives aren't always quite so standardized.

. . . the layout of a kitchen will be determined to a great extent on the available space and on the position of the plumbing, windows, and doors.

. . . kitchen retailers will plan your room for you, but don't always assume they know best. Their job is to sell as many cabinets as possible, so they will often over-prescribe in the storage department.

. . . if you want your kitchen to be a sociable area, it may be better to have fewer cabinets and a large table. This can serve as work surface and storage area, as well as for entertaining or as an office space.

DID YOU KNOW THAT...?

. . . advanced production techniques together with an expanding market have made materials that were once deemed luxurious, and therefore expensive, widely available at realistic prices.

. . . limestone, slate, and terrazzo are now available in thinner, less expensive, tiles, which are equally suitable for walls, countertops, and floors.

. . . convincing imitations of luxury materials such as stone, in the form of less costly ceramic tiles and laminates, are now widespread.

. . . new manufacturing processes have put solid wooden countertops within reach of those on smaller budgets. Provided you treat them regularly with oil, they will last for years.

. . . the disadvantage of laminated cabinets has always been the edges, where poor joining and a tendency to chip eventually show up their shortcomings. New techniques for spray-coating fiberboard now give a better, longer-lasting finish.

. . . etched glass looks sophisticated and modern and is being used very successfully, even at the less expensive end of the market.

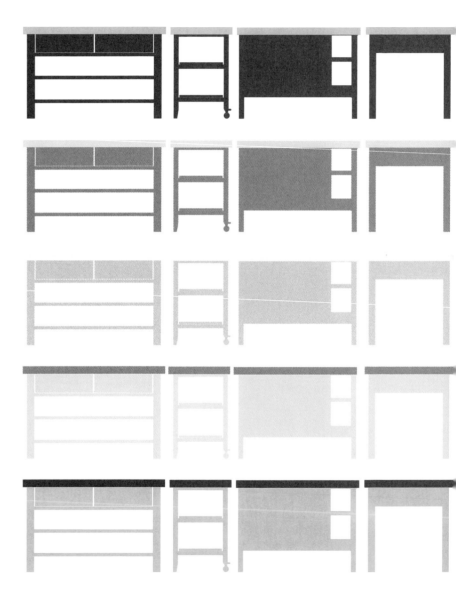

don't throw out the kitchen with the dishwashing water

A new layout doesn't necessarily mean throwing everything out and starting again—it's wasteful, as well as ecologically unsound (see page 288). Faced with a kitchen full of cabinets that aren't in the best state of repair or that just look tired and dated, why not redesign the space using only the good stuff and then smarten it all up with a new countertop? An extra-thick, good-quality countertop can make ordinary cabinets look expensive and can pull a motley collection of fittings into some sort of order. Similarly, you can revive and restore doors and drawer fronts with paint or stain (see pages 166–167) and with new knobs and handles (see pages 168–169).

door + drawer face-lifts
1 **paint + stain**

A paint or stain face-lift will work well only if you take care, so remove all hinges and handles, and prepare the surfaces correctly.

There are now primers that ensure that paint will stick to shiny, nonporous surfaces. This means you can even paint over laminates.

Do a good paint job, and don't forget—you should

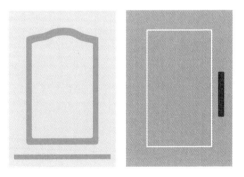

thrifty kitchens + bathrooms

paint both sides of the doors.

You can update old, solid wooden cabinets with a dramatic dark stain, but you'll have to sand off any varnish first. You also need to apply the stain with great care to avoid getting a patchy look.

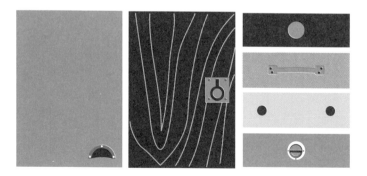

door + drawer face-lifts
2 knobs + handles

Choose your new knobs and handles from the huge ranges at the large home centers and furniture chains, as well as at more specialist stores.

In addition to modern, minimalist knobs and handles —which will add class to any dull kitchen or bathroom cabinet—look for retro plastic and chunky rustic.

Dare to be different by using decorated porcelain or even antique knobs, if you can find them.

Simple metal pull handles and locker fittings look extremely shipshape and streamlined.

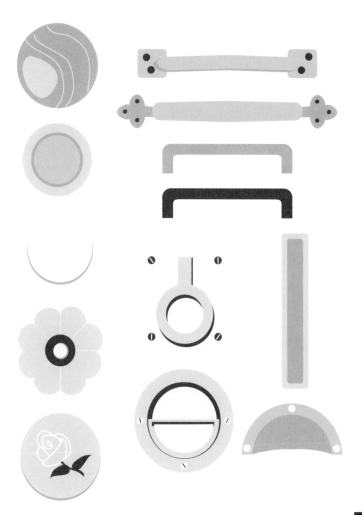

cover + go hang

CURTAINS

If you can't afford or don't want base units in your kitchen, a curtain can hide any appliances and open shelves. Gathered gingham looks nostalgic, and a flowery print looks downright pretty. Straight panels of solid-colored or striped linen or cotton with eyelets along the top edge that are threaded on a metal rod look minimalist and modern.

POLES AND HOOKS

Fix a long metal pole to span the width of a narrow kitchen or kitchen alcove. Then buy a batch of butcher's hooks, hook them on, and hang up all your pots, pans, utensils, dish towels, and aprons.

HANGING BAGS AND BASKETS

Hanging bags and baskets provide extra space for storing fruit and vegetables, plastic bags, kitchen paperware and other sundries.

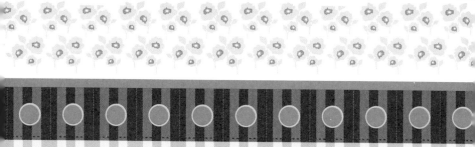

alternative kitchen thinking

If your existing kitchen is a bit of a disaster and you can't afford to have a nice new one built in, try a different approach and go for an eclectic kitchen (sometimes called a European-style kitchen). This kind of kitchen is composed of miscellaneous items of furniture—tables, freestanding cabinets and shelves, maybe a dresser or sideboard—as well as your appliances and sink, of course. With a little flair and imagination, you can create a kitchen of great charm and character, and for relatively little cost.

ECLECTIC

The great economic advantage of an eclectic kitchen is that you don't have to pay for it all at once. You can put together a mixture of new pieces, inherited favorites, and finds garnered from bargain-hunting forays to make your own idiosyncratic style. What's more, with this kind of kitchen you can move the furniture around to suit any changing circumstances or simply on a whim.

CATERING STYLE

Stainless-steel, high-quality catering cabinets cost a fraction of the price of the upscale domestic versions. They're normally very practical and unfussy in design, but bear in mind that they're for restaurant and school-kitchen use, so they're quite large. Buy new direct from catering suppliers—you may have to persuade them to accept a small order—or old from secondhand furniture and office suppliers.

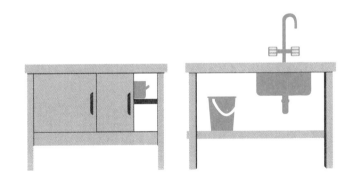

LOCKERS

Fitting lots of smaller cabinets in your kitchen avoids wasting any space, as well as cutting down the time you'll spend rummaging around at the back of a large cabinet for lost ingredients. Lockers are an unusual and efficient alternative to standard kitchen cabinets. They tend to be narrower than standard cabinets so they make good use of small spaces. Available in metal or wood, they can be bought new from some furniture chain stores. Or keep a lookout for old office and school equipment.

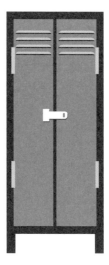

MIX + MATCH

Choosing an eclectic-style kitchen makes for a more personal, characterful, and possibly cheaper decorating scheme. All sorts of chests of drawers, large cupboards and dressers are great for storage. One large cupboard can house everything including pots, pans, china, equipment, and food. A redundant chest of drawers makes the perfect place for storing a wide variety of stuff, from notebooks and crayons to "unruly" ingredients, such as packages of rice, legumes, and pasta.

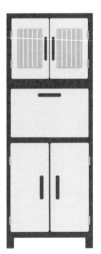

kitchens + another space

The tendency toward fewer, bigger rooms, instead of more, smaller ones, has meant fewer activity-specific areas and more multifunctional rooms. Kitchens are no longer just places for cooking, but places for work and socializing, too. It can be a tight squeeze, but many people are choosing to create an open-plan combination kitchen area.

+ DINE

In a small kitchen, a fold-down table and a couple of stools hung on the wall will free up space for cooking but will allow you to eat in comfort.

A countertop eating area is easy to fit in and can be fixed at normal table- or bar-height. If there's no room for a wide farmhouse-style table, choose one that's long and narrow, and use benches instead of chairs.

+ WORK

A kitchen can be a good place for a bit of peace and quiet, which makes it the ideal environment in which to work. Whether you use it for doing homework, paying the bills, or even earning a living, a kitchen work space can consist of a table that doubles as a desk, a designated section of countertop with space underneath for a stool, or a whole mini-office in a cabinet to protect the computer and other equipment from steam. Even a fold-down table will provide enough space for a laptop computer.

+ LIVE

Kitchens can be cozy, sociable places and are the perfect place for a sofa, armchairs, the TV, and a music system. If space is a problem, it may be possible to squeeze in just one armchair (why not make it a rocking chair?) or build in a bench or window seat. Failing that, have dining chairs that are comfortable enough for prolonged stays.

+ PLAY

Even if you have a large living room, chances are that children will end up around your feet when you're in the kitchen. If you're knocking two rooms together, think about making space next to the kitchen to create a play area where you can keep an eye on the children while you're getting on with the chores. Keep small children safe from kitchen dangers by penning them in with a gate or low partition wall.

+ ACTIVE

For a kitchen that turns into a studio for painting, pottery, or other artistic pursuits, keep surfaces clear and easy to clean. A double sink minimizes the risk of unsuitable or dangerous ingredients contaminating the family food. A large expanse of kitchen floor can be just the place for yoga or other exercise, while for less active pursuits, such as book club or committee meetings, a large kitchen table is ideal.

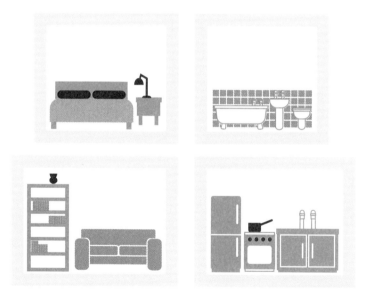

bathroom freshen-ups

Bringing a rather tired and not-very-hygienic-looking bathroom up to scratch does not have to be expensive, provided you aim for pleasant and functional, rather than hip and flashy.

● **COAT OF PAINT**

■ If your bathroom floor, walls, and fixtures are in generally good condition, a coat of paint could be all that's needed to make them look better or even sensational.

■ The bathroom's the one room that's eminently suited to the white-box treatment: a liberal application of brilliant white paint (which could also include the floor) will make the space look and feel fresh and hyper-hygienic.

■ A small bathroom offers the opportunity to go crazy and use intense colors.

● ACCESSORIES

■ The obviously thrifty way to smarten up a lackluster bathroom is with smart accessories. Even the chain stores and supermarkets now sell good-quality bathroom accessories at bargain prices. A new toilet paper holder, towel rod, shower curtain, and toothbrush holder can work wonders, as can a new toilet seat, mirror, and bathroom cabinet. For a modern look, opt for stainless steel and white-coated steel accessories as these work best.

■ A cozy or nostalgic bathroom looks good with wood, especially if it's painted or distressed. Look for small, pretty cabinets and shelves in markets and junk shops.

■ Matching towels smarten up any bathroom, and there's no excuse for even the thriftiest person to hold back from buying them. They can be picked up at very low prices everywhere, including department stores, home centers, and supermarkets.

● IRONY

If you're stuck with hideous wall tiles or colored bathroom fixtures that refuse to look trendy, go for excess. Make a virtue out of necessity, and celebrate those pink tiles by adding extra-fluffy pink towels and a bathmat and outrageous wallpaper featuring cabbage roses or sailing ships. Don't forget to include the bathtub panel in the scheme of things.

● SMALL IS AFFORDABLE

A small space provides the chance to use luxurious materials that would be prohibitively expensive over a large area. Consider limestone, marble, or slate for floors, as well as walls and other surfaces. One roll of expensive but exceptionally beautiful wallpaper will be enough for a small bathroom, and the same goes for a specialist paint in that must-have color.

● TILE TIPS

■ Ceramic tiles are relatively inexpensive, provided you stick to plain ones. Putting them up is a straightforward do-it-yourself job, so long as you buy thin tiles that can be easily cut.

■ Taking off old tiles can be a difficult and messy business, but if you don't want the bother, you can fix new tiles on top of the old.

■ The grouting between tiles tends to become grubby over time, but applying new grouting is simple and cheap. If you want a change, use a contrasting color—white with dark tiles or a soft gray with white are both effective.

●● LIGHT EFFECT

A distinctly average bathroom can be transformed with lighting, but safety is a key issue wherever electricity and water are concerned. Any new light fixtures should be installed by an expert, which could be expensive but may still be cheaper than more drastic improvements. Good lighting is essential for makeup and shaving.

fresh start checklist

If your existing bathroom is beyond the pale, it's often easier to strip everything out and start again. Good-quality, well-designed, simple bathroom suites, comprising a toilet, sink, and bathtub or shower stall, are surprisingly inexpensive, as are faucets and shower fittings.

FLOOR

Take up old floor coverings in the bathroom and check for damp or rot. Bare boards can be painted using gloss or floor paint. A solid wood floor is fine, so long as it's sealed to prevent water damage, but wood laminates aren't recommended, as they tend to lift when wet. Tiles are good, and in a small space you can indulge in luxury limestone, slate, or ceramic. Vinyl is waterproof, but if you plan to do it yourself, cutting and laying it around the fixtures can be tricky. A concrete floor can be sealed and painted with floor paint, but fill in any holes and cracks first.

WALLS

Before painting, papering, or tiling your bathroom walls, seal any damp patches using a proprietary sealant. Latex flat is water resistant; gloss is virtually waterproof (any cracks will affect this); but a buildup of soap isn't easy to remove. Water-resistant, wipe-down wallpaper is quite thick and is good for covering uneven or stained surfaces, but it may start to peel off if the ventilation is poor. Tiles are the perfect wallcovering for bathrooms. So long as you stick to thin, solid-colored tiles, the cost won't be excessive. In a shower area, it's advisable to tile from floor to ceiling, whereas bathtubs and sinks need only a backsplash panel.

VENTILATION

If you have mold, mildew, or fungus in your bathroom, it's probably because of poor ventilation. Opening a window is sometimes all that's needed to solve the problem, but if this doesn't work, you may have to install a fan or vent.

PLUMBING

Moving pipework is costly, but worth the expense if the new layout improves your home. Starting from scratch provides a good opportunity for rerouting and concealing pipework as well as for installing a new bathtub, shower, toilet, or extra sink.

SHOWER VERSUS BATH

While some love a long soak in a bath, others prefer the convenience of a short shower. It's tempting to free up space in a small bathroom by dispensing with the bathtub, but think twice. There are times when a bath is best—bathing young children or soothing tired muscles, for example. When you come to sell your house, the absence of a bathtub could reduce its value. A tub shower is a good compromise, so long as you have a glass screen or generous shower curtain to contain the water. Alternatively, consider a special small bathtub with a seat, which combines bathing and showering.

thrifty kitchens + bathrooms

BATHROOM SUITES

White is best, and simple is even better, especially if your budget is limited. Steel bathtubs are heavier and slightly more expensive than plastic ones, but they're a better buy, since they last longer and don't creak alarmingly when you climb in. Avoid fancy details, such as shell-shaped soap holders and fussy bathtub side panels. Shower floors are normally sold separately and come in a range of sizes. Ceramic is easier to clean, but its weight could be a problem with your ceiling joists.

FAUCETS + FITTINGS

Super-sophisticated faucets and shower fittings can cost a fortune, but there are good, well-designed, modern-looking faucets available at modest prices. Or you could splurge on expensive fittings: the outlay won't be huge, as you will need only one toilet paper holder, a few hooks, and a towel rod.

MIRRORS

Mirrors will make a bathroom feel bigger and more glamorous. Large mirror panels are available in home centers. They enable you to cover a whole wall for a relatively small sum of money.

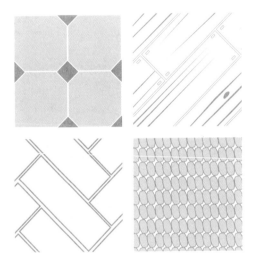

7 **thrifty** floors
\+ walls

floor options

Improve your floor and see the difference it can make. Prices range from cheap to costly, but costly might be worth saving up for.

● STRIP

Bare floors are a stylish option. If you have floorboards that are in good condition, it's relatively easy and inexpensive to strip them and turn them into a fashionable feature. Once they're done, finish them with varnish, wax, or oil.

● PAINT

If the boards are a bit rough, give them a good coating of floor paint, which is hard-wearing and available in many of the trendy colors. It will give a dense, smooth finish that will cover most imperfections.

Better-quality boards look good with a more subtle watercolor approach, using washes of latex flat sealed with robust matte varnish, or waxed and left to acquire a well-worn look. Use light colors, especially if the room is small or dark. Dark or bright colors can look great but could drive you crazy after a while.

● VARNISH + STAIN

If the boards are in good shape and are a pleasing color, all you need is matte varnish for a protective finish and a warm yet clean look. For a dramatic statement, use a dark or colored stain. Exercise caution, though, as this can look oppressive.

● LINOLEUM

In recent years, linoleum has made a comeback. Not to be confused with vinyl, linoleum is made entirely from natural products: linseed oil plus wood or cork powder, ground limestone, and resins. It comes in lovely colors, and in various thicknesses; a thickness of 2 millimeters (just under $1/8$ inch) is suitable for domestic use. Although good-quality linoleum is rather expensive, it makes a beautiful, hard-wearing floor (sheet lino is sturdier than tiles), which should last for many years.

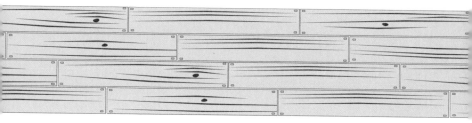

●● TILES

Tiles—and I'm not talking here about vinyl or lino—are very hard-wearing and so make thrifty sense. There's a huge variety on the market, including stone and slate, traditional quarry tiles, and plain or decorated ceramic. Modern, thinner tiles are easier to cut and lay than the old variety, and flexible grouting means that a concrete subfloor is no longer essential.

● LAMINATE FLOORING

This easy-to-lay flooring is very popular and has given homes across the land the "light and airy" feel. Some laminates are extremely cheap, but be careful for the surface is rarely real wood; instead it's a photograph printed onto laminate, which, while convincing, will wear off in a relatively short time in areas of high traffic. Also, floors need to breathe, and many people have discovered that condensation has rotted the joists underneath their "well-fitted" laminate floor.

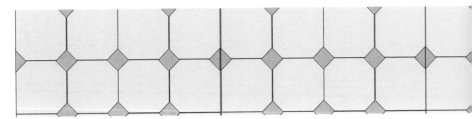

● CARPET

Wall-to-wall carpet is often the cheapest, most sensible option for thrift-minded people; fortunately it's back in fashion. Not only does it cover a multitude of sins, but it's also warm and absorbs sound. Go for a carpet with a high percentage of wool (which looks and feels better than synthetic fibers), in a solid, neutral color that you won't tire of and that will not put off prospective buyers if you try to sell your property.

●●● NATURAL FIBERS

Sisal and other natural fibers are usually rather expensive and need to be glued down to the floor beneath, which adds to the expense. Also they hold dirt and can't be cleaned as easily as soft-pile floor coverings.

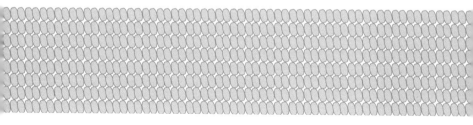

wall options

Walls make up the largest surface area of any room, so what you do with them can make a world of difference to how your room ends up looking.

● WASH + BRUSH UP

Instead of fully repainting a grubby latex painted wall, it's possible to freshen it up using watered-down paint (approximately one part paint to two parts water). Apply with a paintbrush instead of a roller.

● STENCIL

A cheap way to cover a wall with pattern is with stenciling. Exercise subtlety by going for tones of one color or by using related colors, rather than the whole paintbox, and stick to simple designs—avoid the cute and overcomplicated.

● PRIVATE COLLECTION

Turn one wall into a giant scrapbook—the perfect place for all those clippings you've never gotten around to putting in a proper scrapbook. Or use your favorite photographs and postcards. Depending on the state of the wall, attach with tacks or adhesive.

● HANG IT ALL

Wall hangings make great decorations and will conveniently cover up poor or unattractive surfaces. They can add character to a plain room, as well as a bit of extra warmth. What you hang on your wall depends on what you've got—it could be a rug, dhurrie, kilim, embroidered panel, piece of appliqué or patchwork, or just a piece of attractive fabric. It could be home-made or a textile picked up in a souk, ethnic shop, or furniture superstore.

● ALL MAPPED OUT

Maps are large and colorful and are a fairly cheap way of decorating a wall. They're also informative and offer the opportunity to brush up on your geography, plan a trip, or learn more about a place you know and love. World maps tend to be brightly colored with lots of blue sea, but for a more sophisticated effect choose the maps produced by national mapping agencies, such as the U. S. Geological Survey.

wall **trend**

The good news is that wallpaper—perfect for covering poor, uneven surfaces—is back in fashion. The bad news is that the best wallpapers are very expensive. Thrifty options include papering just one wall, finding a lucky bargain in a sale, or using a cheaper paper. This third option is tricky, as it's difficult to find good-quality yet cheap wallpapers. The once-despised palm fronds and spriggy flowers came back into fashion just as they were being banished from the ranges of the mass-market producers and retailers. They have returned, but unfortunately their trendiness comes with a higher price tag.

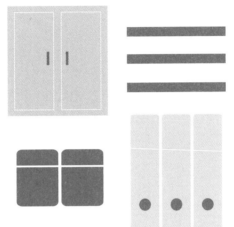

8 thrifty storage

space **shuffle**

De-cluttering is not only fashionable but a good way of reducing the amount of storage you require. Once you've weeded out the unloved, unattractive, and unnecessary, you'll have to accommodate only the things you really want and need.

thrifty storage

DID YOU KNOW THAT...?

. . . rooms with less clutter look bigger. Your kitchen cabinets and drawers should accommodate all your cooking utensils—and possibly your eating utensils, too. If not, could seldom-used items be stored elsewhere? Or could you add a cabinet or two? Similarly, if your clothes closets are bursting and you end up draping garments over chairs or hiding shoes under the bed, it may be time to have some cabinets built in along one wall. (Or get rid of some things!) The same goes for the living room, where built-in cabinets can hide away anything from children's toys to a home office, freeing up the room for more restful or recreational activities in the evening.

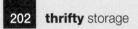

. . . when it comes to displaying your favorite things, discretion and discipline are the buzzwords, so put only good-looking objects out on view. For everything else, think cabinets with plain fronts. These will look like part of the wall and will melt into the background.

. . . narrow, floor-to-ceiling doors for cabinets are very architectural, and they will also help to make a low-ceilinged room look and feel higher.

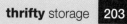

thrifty storage

kitchen **storage** tips

- If an item of kitchen paraphernalia is beautiful or even just pleasing to the eye, why not display it? Packages or cans of food, utensils, and dishes can look attractive, especially when displayed in neat rows or hanging from hooks screwed to the underside of the kitchen shelves.

- Not everything looks good on show though, so stow any unsightly kitchen things away in neat cabinets or—if necessary—on shelves behind a curtain hung from the front edge of the countertop. This is also a good way of disguising a dishwasher.

- In the kitchen it's far easier to pick a mug off a hook or a plate off a plate rack or dresser than it is to delve into a cabinet for it.

up the wall

Simple metal upright-and-bracket shelving systems are readily available and inexpensive. They're easy to fix to the wall and are robust. They're also versatile, as they're suitable for a variety of uses and locations, from hidden-away storage to open display.

Available in white, black, or silver metal finishes, the uprights come in several lengths with a range of bracket sizes for different widths of shelves. The system can be configured to any height and width and can easily be made to fit exactly into alcoves and recesses. The height of the brackets can be adjusted so the shelves can accommodate both short and tall objects. You can also buy dividers and end pieces that will prevent books and objects from toppling over or falling off the ends of the shelves.

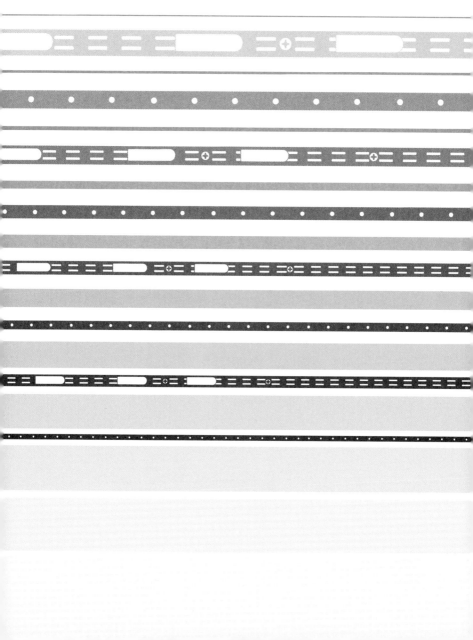

versatile variations

The largest brackets from the upright-and-bracket shelving systems will support a shelf that's deep enough to use as a countertop. Kitchen countertops in wood or laminate work well, but they're heavy, so you'll need to add extra support at the front edge in the form of screw-on legs. If you don't like the way the legs look, cover them with a curtain attached to the underside of the countertop.

Upright-and-bracket systems are also perfect for making an almost-instant, very practical workstation. This could be a stand-alone configuration or might form part of a run of shelves in a kitchen, bedroom, living room, or even a hallway.

For a bedroom, fashion your upright-and-bracket system into a dressing table with extra storage (left). Stow away clothes and accessories in good-looking boxes to keep everything clean and dust-free. Pretty the shelves up with paint, and add a gathered curtain and an upholstered stool.

on the **shelf**

● **LAMINATED BOARD**

This is the least expensive option for making shelves. It consists of particleboard with a laminated coating, usually in white, and is available in a variety of widths. For a smarter, more sophisticated look, fix a batten across the front of the board using finishing nails, then paint or stain the wood to fit in with the rest of your decor.

● **CHUNKY WOOD**

For a more substantial look for your shelves, buy thick planks from a lumber dealer or home center. Sand them down to a smooth finish, then paint, stain, or varnish them to suit.

○ **DRIFTWOOD**

There's no law that says your shelves all have to match, so why not use a collection of reclaimed planks, driftwood, or lucky dumpster finds to create something completely unique?

● **READY-MADE SHELVES**

Some retailers will sell shelving system components separately, so if you covet the look of shelves from an expensive system, you could save money by buying just the shelves. Combine them with less expensive supports, and you'll end up with shelves in a style, material, and finish that might otherwise be beyond your price range.

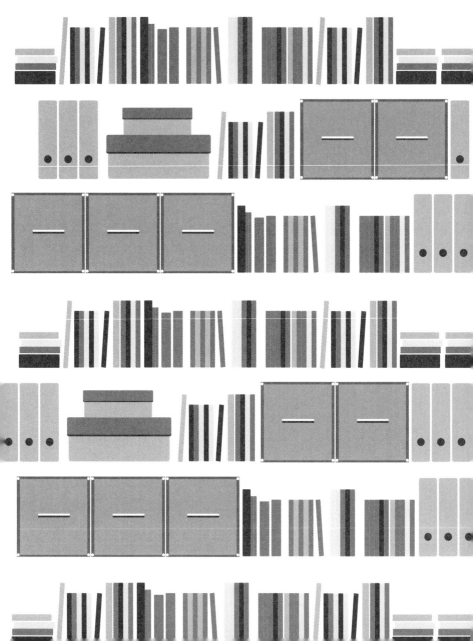

test of **strength**

Before fixing any shelves, make sure your walls can support the weight, especially if they're hollow walls. A shelf full of books, in particular, will be very heavy.

hide**aways**

Incorporate small cabinets into a shelving system to provide concealed storage for less attractive things. Alternatively, choose glass cabinet doors for the opportunity to display a precious item.

on your **own** two feet

■ If your walls aren't up to it, or if you can't or aren't allowed to drill into them, there are plenty of freestanding shelving systems and bookcases to choose from that come in a wide range of materials, dimensions, and configurations.

■ Some of the cheapest freestanding shelf units consist of softwood uprights with softwood shelves. They can look a bit utilitarian but are easily smartened up with paint or stain.

■ If you like the industrial look, opt for galvanized freestanding shelf units—the kind originally intended for garages and utility rooms.

■ Freestanding bookshelves in laminate are very inexpensive; and provided you use them confidently, preferably in a row of two or more, they look fine, especially once they're filled.

■ Solid wood bookcases can be stained, painted, or polished. If you want to hide things away for aesthetic or practical reasons, you could rig up a roller shade in front or, for a cozy cottage look, a floral print curtain.

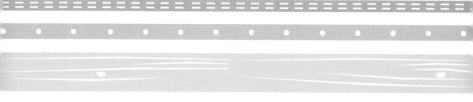

lateral thinking

Not all storage has to be of the shelf or cabinet variety. There are plenty of more unusual storage options to consider, too.

CHESTS, BOXES, + TRUNKS

One large chest can hold a lot of stuff and can also be used as a seat, table, or surface for display. It's ideal for linens and clothes, but keep moths at bay with lavender or old-fashioned mothballs. It's also great for stowing away unsightly equipment and tools. Give beautiful examples pride of place; disguise the more prosaic with a coat of paint or a colorful throw.

BAGS + BASKETS

Many girls have a weakness for bags and can't resist buying more. Use them for storage, hang them up Shaker-style on hooks, or arrange them decoratively on shelves, floors, or the tops of cabinets. They're good for storing anything, including laundry, scarves, gloves, socks and shoes, pants and pantyhose, towels, and toys.

SUITCASES + HAMPERS

Old suitcases aren't great for taking on vacation, but they're perfect for storing anything from clothes to photographs. While old suitcases have charm, new ones can be very chic, too. Decant their contents into garbage bags when you need them for trips away.

storage **"solutions"**

Storage can be a big problem, but it's also big business. There's no shortage of storage "solutions" on the market that promise to bring stylish order to your life. But before you give in to temptation and buy a huge quantity of beautiful boxes or baskets, think carefully. Some so-called storage solutions often take up a lot of room and can become a storage problem in themselves. What's more, they can encourage you to keep things that would be better thrown away.

thrifty storage **217**

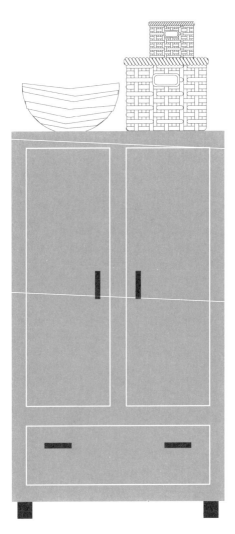

closet creativity

Few people have all the closet space they need. Even a capacious walk-in closet can quickly become overloaded. In such cases, a closet organizer—a system of shelves, rods, and drawers designed to hold clothes and accessories with optimum use of space—is the ideal solution. Or maybe all you need is an extra rod or two, so that you can hang short garments in two tiers. If you've got a serious overflow, consider adding an armoire. These can often be found in secondhand and antique shops and can be attractive features in their own right.

a **grand** entrance

No hall closet? Making do with an unsightly overloaded coatrack with boots scattered underneath? Here again, an armoire could be the answer. If it has shelves for scarves, hats, and other accessories, so much the better. If not, add one of those canvas hanging shelves inside for just such a purpose. You can use the space on top of the armoire for storage, too—perhaps putting a colorful basket up there to hold seasonal accessories.

built-**ins**

■ ●● Manufactured closet organizers come in a wide range of styles and prices. If your budget doesn't run to the deluxe quality, this doesn't matter much, since the shelves. etc., won't be on view except when the closet door is open. But unless you're skilled at d.i.y., it's wise to get a carpenter to install it to make sure everything fits properly.

■ ●●● If you have particular storage needs and are planning on staying in your home for a long time, it's worth saving up for good-quality, ready-made built-in storage or having some custom made. Built-in storage keeps things looking calm and under control, even if there's complete chaos inside.

● **THRIFTY ALTERNATIVE**

In a bedroom, you can create a relaxed effect by covering alcoves or a whole wall of shelving and hanging space with roller or bamboo shades, or simply with a curtain.

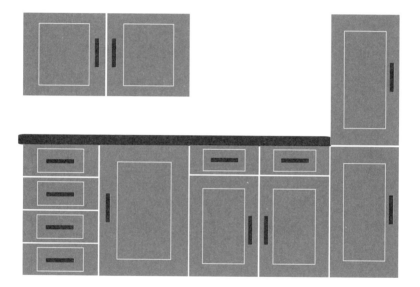

9 **thrifty** furniture fixes

bag a bargain

Just a little damage can reduce the value of a piece of old—or even of not-so-old—furniture quite considerably, so look for a slightly damaged piece and you may well have gotten a good bargain. With a little tender loving care, the item can be reborn good as new, or even transformed completely.

to **DIY** or not to **DIY**

Before buying anything damaged, assess what you may be letting yourself in for. If you're handy with tools, you may wish to tackle any repairs yourself, with the help of an instruction book. If the item in question is very beautiful, good quality, a rarity, or an antique, it could be worth enrolling in an evening or day class and learning furniture repairs. That way you will also be able to carry out the repair under the supervision of your teacher. If you are not practical, though, it is advisable to get the job done by a skilled local carpenter or upholsterer. The final cost may still work out less than if you buy the equivalent in good or perfect condition.

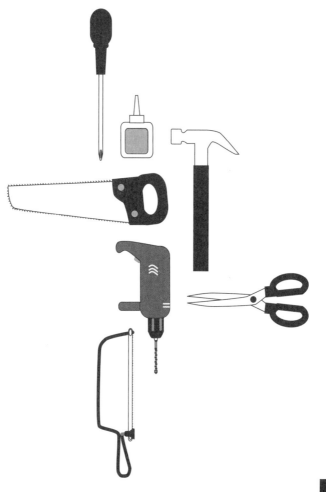

a quick fix or a **pain** in the neck?

- While it's possible to repair damaged veneer, it's a tricky, skilled job.

- Old colored laminates are often chipped and can't be repaired, so you have to decide whether the damage is part of a piece's charm.

- So long as there isn't too much damage to leg ends or to the pieces to be glued, fixing loose joints on a chair is a simple task.

- It isn't particularly easy to replace split or missing drawer bottoms, so think before you buy.

- Provided the frame isn't damaged, a cleanup, some sanding down or planing, and some candle wax applied to the runners will improve the fit of almost all drawers.

- Handles are easy to replace, and new ones can change an item's character if you wish.

- Casters can be replaced—look for old ones in secondhand stores. Seek advice on the best types of glue to use with them.

- A new slipcover and a few tacks may be all that's required to bring a sofa or armchair back to life. But if any springs are sticking through the underside or if there's a serious stuffing deficiency, it will be a bigger, more complex job to put things right.

- Reupholstering dining chairs is a reasonably straightforward job, but when it comes to large sofas and armchairs, buy a do-it-yourself book, take an upholstery class, or have the work done by a trained professional.

- Got an old bed frame? Cover worn-out springs with wooden slats, and replace a saggy old mattress with a new one.

simple chair repairs

The three tools shown opposite on the left will make chair repairs easier. Left, above is a clamp to keep all the pieces in position while the glue dries. Left, center is a small right-angled metal bracket. This can be used to strengthen joints and frames, either as an alternative to gluing or to add extra support. Left, below is a syringe—great for getting glue into nooks and crannies.

Chairs such as this one (1) are usually very cheap and plentiful; and since they're well made and robust they can easily be rehabilitated. Take out the seat pad and clean the frame, stripping off any varnish if necessary. Check all the joints, and if they're loose, glue them in place using a clamp (2). Position the clamp vertically when gluing joints on the chair back. Treat the repaired chair frame with oil or wax. Remove the seat cover, including as many of the old tacks as possible. Add more padding to the seat, if necessary, and cover with new upholstery fabric, pulling it over the frame and tacking it into place underneath (3).

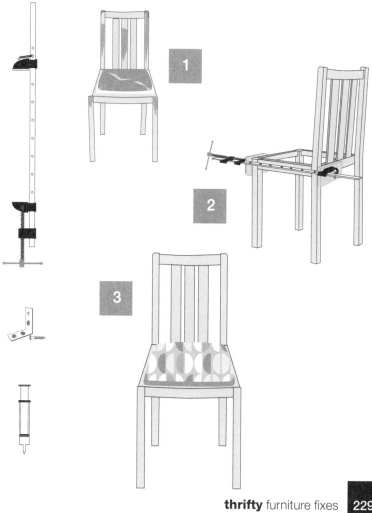

clean wood

■ You can buy proprietary products that are
specially formulated to remove dirt and
discolored wax from wood. Alternatively,
a warm solution of a gentle detergent (eco-
varieties are good) will suffice. Use a soft,
long-bristled brush to get into any nooks and
crannies. For stubborn dirt and stains, use a
scouring pad.

■ Rinse off the soap and dry thoroughly with a
cloth. For a bare-wood finish, apply Danish or
finishing oil or a good-quality wax polish (see
pages 232–234). If you plan to paint the wood,
first apply a coat of primer.

■ For wood that's already painted, apply fresh
paint directly on top of the cleaned surface.

stripped wood

■ Old painted or varnished furniture can be full of charm, but if the wood beneath is beautiful, you might like to liberate it from its suffocating coats of paint or varnish.

■ Stripping is tedious and messy, since it involves the use of caustic chemicals, which are corrosive and give off unpleasant fumes. Be careful.

■ Buy a good product, follow the instructions to the letter, and wear protective gloves, clothing, and the correct type of mask.

■ Don't rush the job, and don't try to remove the paint before it has properly softened, as it will only require more stripper to get all the paint off.

furniture **finishing** touches

There are a confusing number of proprietary products for finishing wood but they're all either wax- or oil-based. Find your way through the maze with this easy summary.

WAXES + OILS

Waxes dry to a hard finish and can be buffed to a shiny coating, which keeps out dirt and protects against scratches. Oil soaks into the wood and gives a soft, matte finish. New softwood, from which much cheap furniture is made, is normally finished with a coat of hard-wearing varnish to protect and color the wood. This coating isn't very flattering and looks cheap. Rubbing with abrasive paper will break down the surface; then you can finish with oil to give the wood a subtler, more natural finish.

 thrifty furniture fixes

DANISH OR FINISHING OIL

These thinnish liquids are easy to apply with a brush or cloth and form a water-resistant surface that prevents the wood from drying out and splitting. Essential for treating new wooden countertops, the oil should be reapplied at regular intervals to keep the wood in good condition. You can also use it on wooden furniture, shelves, and other fittings.

LIQUID WAX

Liquid wax is wax that's been dissolved in solvent, which makes it easier to apply. Most have a stain added—usually light, medium, or dark. Liquid waxes are useful for putting life back into dry wood and for toning down or deepening its color. Some dry to a hard finish, so check the can.

BEESWAX POLISH

The best furniture polish is made from beeswax blended with solvent and perfumed with lavender or lemon. Go for the purest blend, and avoid products containing silicone, as this forms a surface buildup that's difficult to remove.

WOOD STAIN

As the name says, it stains the wood. Choose from light yellow pine to almost-black ebony. Paler tones are safer, but dark stains can look sensational, provided you apply them evenly, which can be tricky over large areas. Once applied, stains can't be removed, so be sure you know what you're letting yourself in for before you start. It pays to check the effect on a hidden corner.

VARNISH

Use clear varnish for a finish that's hard-wearing and waterproof. There are many different types to choose from, but a matte finish looks best. Many varnishes are polyurethane-based, so they'll eventually darken the wood; and if you use them on top of light-colored paint, they'll give it a yellowy tinge. To avoid this, choose an acrylic varnish.

DID YOU KNOW THAT...?

. . . there's a lot of reasonably priced new and secondhand reproduction furniture around, including tables, chairs, and even some quite grand-looking beds. Although the shape and quality are fine, the finish is often crude, which makes it look gauche rather than elegant. However, with a bit of work, repro can be improved.

Remove hard varnished or gilded surfaces using abrasive paper, steel wool, and, if necessary, paint stripper. Use abrasive paper to smooth down and soften any sharp edges, including any decorative moldings. Wash thoroughly and allow to dry before applying wax or oil (see pages 232–234) for a natural finish, or apply a coat of primer, then paint with an eggshell paint. Creamy white or pastel shades look the most elegant.

paint possibilities

- Old or new, prosaic or characterful, tables, armoires, chests of drawers, trunks, bookcases, and shelves can all be transformed and rehabilitated with a coat of paint.

- Wood finishes, particularly on new furniture, can vary widely in color and this can make a collection of pieces bought from different places look a mishmash. Painting them all the same color or shades of one color, brings unity.

- It's a well-known fact that painting a jumble of odd chairs the same color will create a quirky but matching set. But, equally, a matching set of very ordinary chairs can be enlivened by painting them all in different colors.

- A thick coating of white gloss paint disciplines even the scruffiest piece of furniture, Dull matte white is an even more sophisticated option.

- Convert starkly new into convincingly old using simple but effective paint effects such as crackle glaze or distressing (see page 239).

thrifty furniture fixes 237

furniture paint **roundup**

GLOSS PAINT

Before using on bare wood, apply a primer; and for
an even, hard-wearing finish, follow with an undercoat
or a coat of latex flat. Then apply two or more coats
of gloss. Rub down between each coat with fine steel
wool or abrasive paper.

LATEX FLAT

Besides being cheaper than gloss or eggshell, latex
flat paint is easier to use. Though not as robust, it can
be used on furniture, provided you seal it with either
clear varnish or wax polish (see pages 232–234).
Beeswax polish gives a soft sheen finish, which will
improve and harden with regular polishing.

SPECIALIST PAINTS

Many specialist paints are based on old, traditional
recipes and are made from natural ingredients. Not
only do they have an intensity of color and a subtlety
and finish that aren't possible with chemically based
paints, but they're also healthier, because they're low
in VOCs (Volatile Organic Compounds). Casein paints
(based on the old milk paints) have a soft, chalky
finish, which, when used on furniture, will need to be

finished with a coat of acrylic varnish. Eggshell gives a soft sheen, and dead-flat oil paint has a dense, matte finish. Water-based versions of eggshell and gloss are also available.

CRACKLE GLAZE

Crackle-effect products give a finish that ranges from quite crude to very subtle. The method of application varies according to the brand, but the process involves painting a glaze over paint—latex flat goes on easier and dries quicker—which causes the paint to craze. Then you rub on paint or wax in a darker color to emphasize the crackle lines.

DISTRESSING

For a worn look on furniture or woodwork, apply a coat of paint followed by a coat of a different color. Then, using fine steel wool, rub off some of the top coat along the edges and on other areas of high wear. Alternatively, after applying the first coat of paint, rub the edges and patches with a wax candle, so that these resist the second coat. To give the appearance of several layers of old, chipped paint, continue the process using a different color each time.

10 **thrifty** window treatments

The idea that one must use only decorator fabrics for draperies or curtains has long gone out of the window. Nowadays anything goes, so it's your chance to be imaginative as well as thrifty.

● PLAIN . . .

Simple panel curtains, with little or no gathering or pleating and hung from plain rods, are not only easy to make but use the minimum amount of fabric. The very simplest consist of a piece of unhemmed fabric hung from a bamboo cane or tensioned steel cable.

● . . . OR FANCY?

Check out salesrooms, secondhand outlets, and estate sales, where you may find elaborate draperies that can be taken apart and made into less fussy creations. Alternatively, use the elaborate versions in all their glory and make them the star attraction in an otherwise plain room. You may be lucky enough to find swags and cascades in velvets, damasks, and even chintz.

don't **bare** all

Bare windows may be fashionable—as well as being the ultimate thrifty solution—but unless you're lucky enough not to be overlooked, it may not be your best option. What is more, the bare look can feel cold. Draperies, shades, and blinds, on the other hand, screen out drafts and prying eyes and can be used to complement and complete your decor.

PORTIÈRE RODS

These hinged curtain rods (opposite, right) are useful for flat window panels—an extremely thrifty form of window treatment. A single one can also be used for the original purpose: to hang a curtain over a door (*porte* in French) to keep out drafts. They're hard to find, but try the Internet.

CAFÉ CONTINENTAL

A scrap of pretty fabric clipped to a length of tensioned steel cable wire (below, right) with clothespins is all you need.

MIX AND MATCH

You may not have enough precious vintage fabric to curtain an entire window, so don't be afraid to mix and match. Either stitch pieces together or thread a collection of different pieces on the same curtain rod.

BOLD BORDERS

Liven up an otherwise plain pair of curtains or draperies with a border of a special or extravagant fabric (below, left).

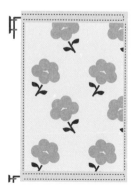

FLIMSY CURTAIN

Gather a filmy fabric "skirt" to a heavier fabric top that's strong enough to take the curtain hardware (below, right).

FOLD-BACK PANELS

Hang a plain panel from simple hooks and eyelets. Fold the panel back to reveal a contrasting lining (opposite, left).

LACE PANEL

Try a single lace panel. It can be dyed for extra impact.

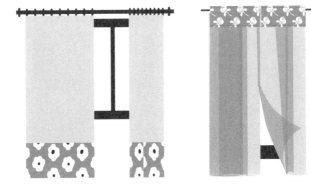

 thrifty window treatments

LAYER CURTAINS

Size doesn't always matter, especially if you're prepared to mix, match, and use your imagination. Try a pair of long curtains or draperies in one fabric hung next to the window and a pair of short ones in a totally different fabric hung on top from a second rod.

THERMAL

Keep out winter winds (and reduce your heating bills) with quilted, padded, or thick, lined draperies. Put a layer of batting between two different fabrics, and quilt them, either with a sewing machine or by hand, using a few knotted stitches here and there. Or simply hang a pretty quilt at the window (below, right).

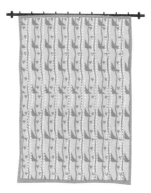

thrifty window treatments

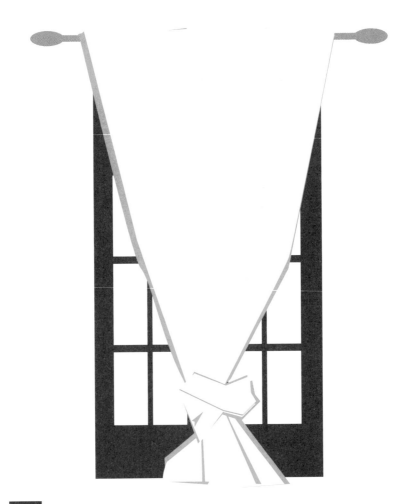

make-do **curtains**

If you don't want to, or can't, sew, make curtains from sheets, tablecloths, quilts (see page 247), throws, or dhurries, all of which have ready-finished edges. Or simply use lengths of fabric with a selvage.

SHEETS
An old linen sheet draped over a pole looks dramatic and adds a hint of grandeur.

TABLECLOTHS
Small, lightweight tablecloths can easily be hung from clip-on or sew-on curtain rings. Crisp, white embroidered tablecloths look especially pretty in bedrooms and bathrooms.

DHURRIES
Inexpensive dhurries make great window coverings. Hang from a pole and make a feature of the fringe.

FABRIC OPULENCE
Generous lengths of old velvet or damask will add a dash of opulence to a room.

how do you **measure** up?

Because there's now a more relaxed attitude to drapery/curtain widths and lengths, measuring your windows doesn't have to be so precise. The thrifty bonus is that the fashion for a simpler look with minimal gathering means that less fabric is required.

If you choose a patterned fabric with an obvious horizontal design, you should match the pattern across both panels; otherwise it will look odd. Similarly, if you're joining more than one width of fabric to make a single panel, it will look better if you match the pattern along the seam. Don't forget to buy extra fabric to allow for the pattern repeat—a lot of stores state the length of the repeat, which will help you calculate how much fabric you need.

● **THE PERSONAL TOUCH**

If you don't want the bother of making curtains or draperies, go for ready-made. Some are great value and can be personalized with borders, appliqué or crochet flowers, patchwork panels, fringe, or buttons and bows. Inexpensive lightweight, off-the-rack curtains also make pretty linings for draperies.

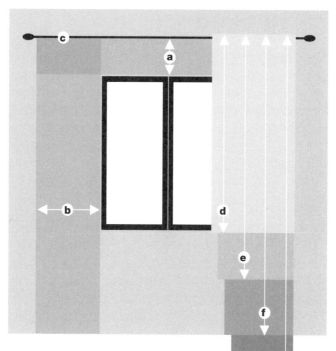

a height at which you hang the rod; don't forget to allow for a gap between the rod and the curtain

b allow enough room for the draperies/curtains to pull back away from the window

c curtain/drapery hardware

d sill-length

e cropped

f floor-length

g extra-long

get **hooked**

The range of hooks and rings for hanging curtains and draperies is wide. Whether your choose sew-in curtain rings, clip-on hooks, or eyelets depends on the weight of your curtains and your choice of rod. Eyelets don't require any hooks, because they thread directly onto the rod. Just make sure the eyelets are big enough for the rod though!

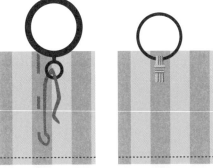

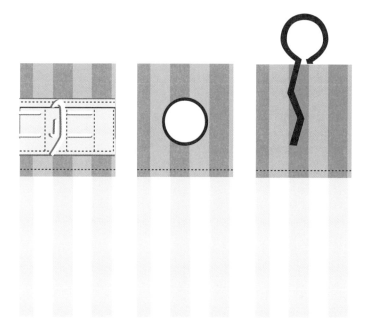

hang it all

● BAMBOO CANES
Very cheap and available in a range of lengths from garden centers.

● TACKS
For an impromptu curtain, attach fabric to the window frame using thumbtacks.

● WOODEN DOWELS
Thin lengths work for lightweight curtains and the thickest, with the right supports, for heavy draperies.

● PIPING
Use copper and plastic piping fixed to the wall with plumbers' fittings.

● BULLDOG CLIPS
Good for no-fuss curtain hanging. Thread or clip onto string, cord, or wire.

● WIRE
Steel cable, strung between eyelet hooks and held taut by tensioners, looks smart, minimalist and modern.

thrifty window treatments

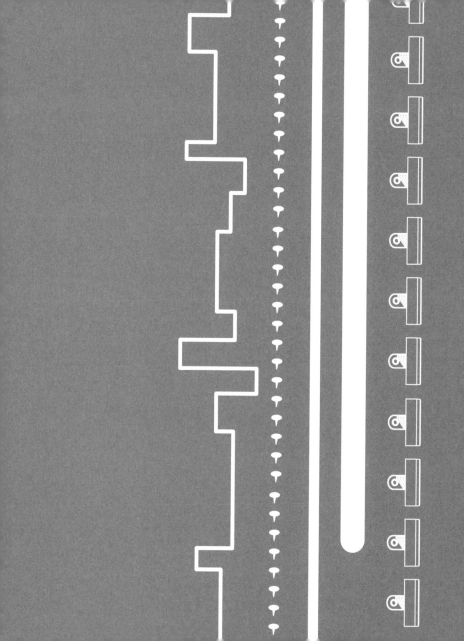

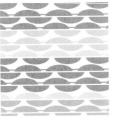

11 thrifty projects

the **joy** of fabric

Fabrics give an interior warmth and character and, depending on your preferences, can be a barely noticeable presence or a striking main feature. Make the most of fabrics if you'd like to detract from unattractive surroundings, disguise ugly furnishings, or hide equipment, appliances, or just a mess.

DID YOU KNOW THAT...?

. . . you can use a limited collection of fabrics to cover a motley assortment of upholstered furniture, so that it all looks as though it belongs together. But avoid an excessively coordinated look by choosing a variety of tones and textures. You could perhaps also include a smattering of pattern.

DID YOU KNOW THAT...?

. . . retailers can sell upholstered furniture only if the fabric conforms to fire-risk regulations and comes with the appropriate certificate. The same is true of fabric used by professional upholsterers. This doesn't apply to homemade slipcovers, though, so if you're making your own and using nonregulation fabric, check the small print of your buildings and contents insurance policy.

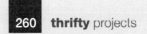

make a **statement**

If you've seen a beautiful but expensive fabric that you really can't live without, don't despair. Just use a small quantity made into a short, ungathered curtain, a simple shade, a single chair cover or an individual throw pillow. The amount used may be small, but it will still make a statement in your room.

fabric file

Whether you want a dash or a splash, fabrics are the perfect way to add color, pattern, and texture to a room. Even a small length can have a big impact.

NATURAL FIBERS

Plain linens and cottons, including denim, are great for everything from upholstery to curtains and draperies, and they can usually be easily washed to keep them looking good. What's more, the texture of crunchy cotton and linen weaves will add some variety to your decorative scheme.

WOOLS

Wool tweed, suiting, and cashmere are smart and warm alternatives for draperies and shades; but be aware that they often require specialist cleaning.

TRADITIONAL PRINTS

Chintz and toile de Jouy look cozy in a traditional way, while spriggy flowers have a fresh appeal. Provençal prints are bright and cheerful and can be picked up for little cost. They make great curtains, tablecloths, and bedcovers.

LUXURY

Velvets, silks, and damasks add glamour. Use them for lavish draperies or throws.

BOLD PRINTS

Let these take center stage in a simple setting. If you're nervous of using them in quantity, limit them to just a pillow or a shade.

REMNANTS

Use odd fabric lengths, remnants, and scraps of fabric to make patchwork throws and covers for beds or pillows.

trimmings **treat**

Fancy trimmings are expensive, especially when it takes several yards to trim a pair of draperies or a bedcover, but there are thrifty ways of making great trims that will help to brighten up or glamorize the mundane.

CROCHET FLOWERS

While away a few relaxing hours making crochet flowers. Use up odd balls of yarn bought in sales or from thrift shops.

POMPOMS

Relive your childhood by winding yarn around a pair of cardboard circles to make pompoms.

KNITTED TRIMS

Knit your own trims. Cast on a small number of simple stitches and just keep going.

BLANKET STITCH

Add blanket stitch around the edges using a big needle and thick yarn in a contrasting or subtly similar color.

BINDING

Bind edges with strips of printed fabric. Ideal for using up scraps, remnants, material from old clothes, and small but fabulous pieces of vintage fabric.

RECYCLE

Salvage fringe, lace, buttons, and ribbons from old clothes, bedspreads, linens, cushions, shawls, scarves and lampshades. You can even reuse pockets.

to **sew** . . .

■ Make a throw using two inexpensive fabrics, one printed and one solid-colored. Sandwich a very cheap fleece blanket between them to give a quilted look as well as extra warmth. You can achieve a real quilted effect with simple straight lines of stitching or, if you're feeling inspired, with more decorative stitching.

■ Antique embroidered napkins and lacy doilies are charming and can often be picked up for next to nothing. Sew two napkins together to make a pretty cover for a small pillow, or stitch a lacy doily on top of a crunchy linen or starched cotton pillow cover.

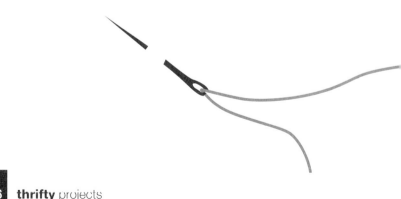

thrifty projects

■ Although threadbare patches on sofas and chairs can add charm, they reduce the life of the furniture, so get out your sewing kit and get patching. A spare piece of matching fabric makes the perfect patch, but if you'd like a funky look, a contrasting pattern or piece of solid-colored, contrasting fabric will do nicely, too.

. . . or **not** to sew

■ Layer your bed with throws, blankets, and bedspreads. Don't be afraid to mix the very expensive with the dirt cheap.

■ An old embroidered tablecloth thrown over a bed turns a cheap plain cotton bedspread into a vintage treasure.

■ Wrap up furniture in chunky knits, crochet, fleeces, sheepskins, tartan rugs, and the more subtle fake furs. Add pillows in knits, denim, cords, and shaggy wools.

■ Evoke an aura of opulence with kilims, thin Persian-style carpets, and pashminas. Add an Eastern influence with jewel-colored silks and a few tassels and fringes.

■ Drape fringed silk shawls over a sofa or, better still, over a chaise longue. Wake up tired chairs with glamorous crushed velvet throws. Finish with touches of silk, satin, and lace in the form of pillows and trims.

- Silk-lined walls may be a bit excessive; but if you covet fabric on the walls, you can have a fabric wall hanging, or you could tack the fabric to the wall to make a more permanent feature.

- Why not hang bed curtains from a pole screwed into the ceiling? Light, floaty curtains are romantic, but damask or velvet will add a touch of warmth and a sense of history.

- Gathered bed skirts look a bit passé; new ones are tailored to hang straight. If you don't want the bother of sewing a bed skirt, simply use a throw, sheet, blanket, or quilt thrown over the box spring, underneath the mattress. Use as part of a layered look, mixing a number of patterns, textures, and colors as you add throws, coverlets, and pillows on top of the mattress.

crochet revival

Crochet is very much in vogue, so old crocheted cushions and blankets are quickly snapped up in rummage sales and thrift shops. Picking up some yarn and a crochet hook and doing the crochet yourself (or asking someone else to do it for you) is the next best thing. It's fun and easy and gives you an excuse to buy some of the fabulous new yarns that are now available in stores.

prudent **patchwork**

Patchwork is popular, but ready-made items can be pricey. The thrifty alternative is to take up this enjoyable and relaxing pastime and make your own much more personal and distinctive items, using remnants, scraps, and favorite old clothes. Start small by making a pillow cover.

headboard special

■ ● A padded headboard is relatively simple to make using a piece of chipboard covered with fabric, with a layer of padding underneath for comfort. Make the headboard a little wider than the bed and as tall as you like. When calculating the amount of padding and fabric you need, allow for the size of the board plus at least 6 inches all the way around. Lightly sand the edges of the board to prevent damage to the fabric. Cover one face of the board with thick batting or fleece, and secure it at the back with staples or small tacks. Next, cover the padding with your fabric, using staples or larger-headed tacks. To hang the board securely on the wall, use concealed fixings set into the back. Fix it on the wall at mattress height or at baseboard level.

■ ● You can make a lightweight headboard using ready-stretched canvas from an art supplies store. If they don't stock canvases wide enough for a full-size bed, you can buy artist's canvas by the yard and make your own frame using ready-cut stretchers, which easily slot together. Stretching the canvas tightly and neatly requires care and skill. The final look is up to you and your artistic aspirations. You can leave the canvas blank, paint a picture on it, or commission a picture from a friendly neighborhood artist.

● Plain bed frames are cheap enough, but sometimes they're a little characterless, not to mention hard on the head when you are reading in bed. You can soften them by draping a quilt over the headboard. Old quilts look the part, but there are plenty of pretty new quilts in stores at reasonable prices.

● For a casual, arty look, simply pin a rectangle of fabric behind the bed. Coarse linen looks suitably austere, but a scrap of velvet or damask adds a dash of unconventionality. For a smarter, more permanent look, hem along the edges, fix eyelets along the top, and hang from hooks screwed into a batten fixed to the wall.

chair **flair**

Need to brighten up a chair? All you need is a small amount of woven or knitted fabric, and you can have a whole new look—and at bargain-basement prices, too.

SAVE IT

The backs and arms of armchairs are vulnerable to dirt and wear. This modern take (below, left) on traditional antimacassars and arm protectors adds a crisp, clean set of collar and cuffs to protect a new chair or to cover the grubbiest parts of an old one.

FASHION ITEM

The fashion for ponchos comes and goes. While they're out of favor, why not make good use of them on a chair back (opposite, right)?

OFFICE WEAR

Office chairs don't have to wear work clothes. You could dress them to blend in with their surroundings, but why not go for something rather more unsuitable (below, left)?

BOBBLE HAT

A silly wooly hat will brighten up a plain chair and somebody's day (below, right). Get knitting.

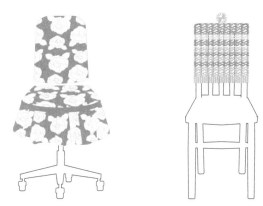

COVER-ALL

Making tie-on covers (below, left) for an old wooden armchair is relatively easy. They can be removed for washing or whenever you fancy a change of style.

TWO-PIECE

Pop a simple slipcover over a chair back, add a covered cushion to the seat, and, depending on the fabric, you can turn an ordinary chair into a retro piece (below, right) or into something altogether more refined.

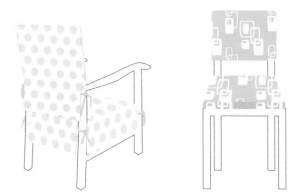

SEMIFITTED

For a semifitted chair cushion cover, cut enough fabric to cover the seat, to allow for a generous border, and for rounding off the front corners. Hem along the edges and thread elastic through (below, left).

ADDED COMFORT

Folding chairs are a great invention, but the seat back can be uncomfortable. A small sewn pad folded over and fixed with snap fasteners to the chair back makes a world of difference (below, right).

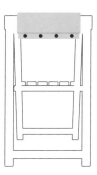

cover up

Making slipcovers can be complicated, especially if your chair is curvy. Precisely fitting covers take time and skill but more casual covers are now in vogue, and they're a lot easier to make.

The slipcover shown on pages 280–281 has been pared down to the simplest shapes and the minimum number of pieces and doesn't have too many curves. It's relatively simple to make, but take care. Remember: measure twice, cut once!

Use the two diagrams at the top of page 280 to show you which pattern pieces you need. The best way to mark the shape of the pieces is to lay the fabric, wrong side out, over the chair and mark with tailor's chalk. Cut out the pieces on a flat surface or in situ on the chair. Don't forget to leave a seam allowance of approximately 1 inch along all edges.

The diagram at the bottom of page 280 indicates how all the pieces fit together, but it isn't a cutting pattern, because that depends on the shape of your chair. Plan the most economical way of using your fabric, allowing for matching the pattern if necessary.

Stitch A to B along the top straight edge. Place wrong side out on the chair and pin C1 and C2 to the sides of B. Sew in place. Pin, baste, and stitch the curved seam joining C1 and C2 to A (Fig. 1, page 281).

Place the cover over the chair. Pin and baste piece E to piece A across the top and to C1 and C2 at the sides. Pin and baste D1 and D2 to C1 and C2. Remove the cover and stitch (Fig. 2, page 281).

Turn the cover right side out and place over the chair. Either leave with simple seams or add a row of topstitching on the right side, around the back and arms, to add definition (Fig. 3, page 281).

FABRIC CHOICE

A heavy, hard-wearing, closely woven fabric is usually recommended, but this is difficult to handle, and many ordinary domestic sewing machines cannot cope with it. Using a medium-weight cotton or linen is fine, so long as it isn't too flimsy and doesn't fray easily.

Wash your fabric before sewing, as many fabrics shrink. If you're not careful, after its first wash your cover may fit too snugly—or not at all.

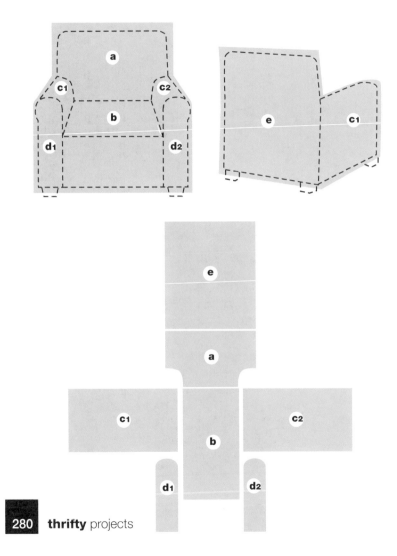

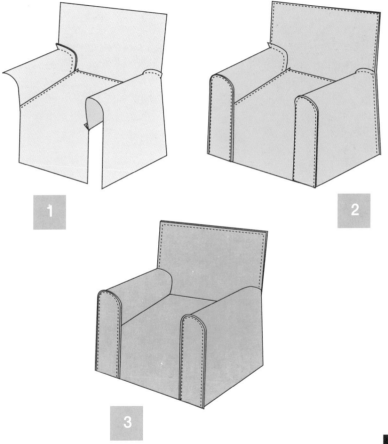

1

2

3

cheapskate choice for shelving

Shelving made from planks and bricks is a good thrift idea and is perfect for the "industrial" look, especially if you use scaffolding planks. Once a cliché, this simple construction is back in fashion. It doesn't need to be fixed to the wall, but stability is crucial, so make sure you use enough bricks to form a stable construction. Bricks are heavy, so if you're worried about the weight on your floor, don't build too high.

DIY **art**

Commissioning a family portrait can be expensive, but is a great investment. If funds are low, you could always have a try yourself. Why not scan in a photograph and play around with it on a computer or photocopier? You might produce your own version of an Andy Warhol or a Cindy Sherman. Better still, equip your five-year-old with brushes, paint, and a huge canvas and you'll have your very own piece of "brat art."

paper pleasures

■ There are some wonderful wallpapers around with huge motifs, so why not cut the motifs out and stick them to a plain armoire to give it a lift (opposite left)? You could use a length left over from a wallpapering job, find a bargain-basement roll or buy a single roll of something elegant. If you dare, just try asking for a sample.

■ Jazz up an inexpensive, plain wooden chest of drawers using a different paper on each drawer front (below).

■ There's no law that says doors have to be plain. If you want only a small amount of pattern in a room, the door's as good a place as any to make your statement (opposite right).

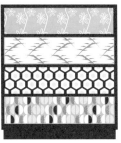

12 eco-thrift

DID YOU KNOW THAT...?

. . . reasons for being thrifty extend beyond your pocket to your personal well-being, as well as to that of the environment. You don't have to be a crank to be aware that we can't continue with the cycle of consuming, throwing away, and consuming afresh that pervades Western society. It may make the economy go round, but it's not so good for the planet. Taking a new look at how you, your nearest and dearest, and your neighbors use the earth's resources could lead to a different way of life altogether.

need a **re**-ason?

RE-DUCE

Reduce your consumption by thinking before you spend your money. What will you gain from the purchase? Try to buy only what you need, rather than what you want.

RE-USE

Don't throw away plastic bags; re-use them as often as possible. Instead of disposables, buy washable cotton diapers, cotton handkerchiefs, and cotton dishcloths, which you can boil up as required to clean and reuse.

RE-CYCLE

Glass, paper, cardboard, plastic, cans, and other items should be recycled through your local government. Some recycling centers and local governments also distribute old computers, electrical appliances, furniture, clothes, and books to good causes. But don't just recycle your trash; buy products made from recycled materials such as glass, paper, and plastic.

RE-VIVE

Reawaken old passions by reviving past interests in

hobbies, sports, artistic activities, and other pastimes. Anything from knitting to kite flying, or jogging to jiving can bring you pleasure and needn't be costly.

RE-INVENT

Besides putting old furniture to new uses and turning old clothes and fabrics into pillows covers and patchwork quilts, think big and reinvent the way you use your home to make it more practical, pleasing, and energy efficient.

RE-FRESH AND RE-INVIGORATE

Tired homes often need little more than a good clean and a coat of paint to reawaken your interest in them. And instead of splurging on something new for the home, reinvigorate it by moving the furniture around.

RE-THINK

Reevaluate the way you live your life, from your diet and dress to your home and work life. Instead of going shopping during your lunch break, visit museums or galleries, where you can often view the permanent collections for free.

RE-CLAIM

Old floorboards, bricks, and window frames can be reused, so either recycle them or sell them on. Reclaimed materials, which are often better quality and nicer looking than their new equivalents, are sometimes cheaper than buying new.

RE-ORGANIZE

Save time, money, and your temper by reorganizing your home, your possessions, and your habits. Make sure there's somewhere to put everything and that anything that's used frequently is kept at hand.

RE-NEW

Buy lumber from renewable resources—look for the FSC mark of the World Wildlife Fund's Forest Stewardship Council.

RE-LAX

Have a night in with a good book, in front of the television or having a chat with family or friends. Eating out is fun but expensive. For the cost of a main course in a restaurant, you could feast on bread, cheeses, meats, and pastries, which don't require any cooking.

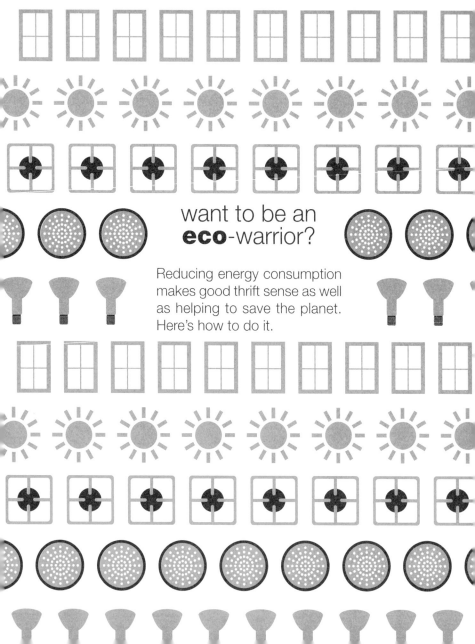

want to be an **eco**-warrior?

Reducing energy consumption makes good thrift sense as well as helping to save the planet. Here's how to do it.

●● ELECTRICAL APPLIANCES

When buying a refrigerator, dishwasher, clothes washer, or other major appliance, choose an Energy Star-rated model. These use less energy and less water. Although Energy Star-rated washing appliances are inherently energy efficient, you should use them with energy efficiency in mind, making sure you're always washing a full load, using a low-temperature wash cycle and, if possible, an economy wash program. You should also turn appliances off completely, as the standby state uses a surprising amount of electricity.

● LIGHTING

Save energy by turning off unnecessary lights and by not leaving lights on in empty rooms. However, do make sure that stairs are well lit. A low level of light can be depressing, as well as bad for the eyes, so use good task lighting for reading, working, and cooking. You should also fit energy-saving bulbs where possible. They use 75 percent less energy and last up to 12 times longer than normal bulbs. They're more expensive, so buy in bulk via mail order to save money.

●● INSULATION

Make sure your home is well insulated. Attic insulation is easy to put in place, but wall insulation isn't so straightforward. However, it's worth considering if you're buying or renovating a home. Flax, cellulose ,and materials made from recycled paper and wool are some eco-options for insulating.

● WINDOWS AND DOORS

You may like bare windows but an enormous amount of heat is lost through glass and badly fitting frames. Thick, generous draperies that cover the whole window frame will not only keep in the heat but also make a room feel warmer, and a curtain over a door will also help to keep out the cold. Velvet or heavy cotton is good, but try a blanket or throw, or a fleece, which is very light and easy to hang in place. You should also fit draft-proofing strips on outside doors and zap any under-door gales with a knitted or woven-fabric dog or snake draft excluder.

eco-thrift

●● FURNACES + RADIATORS

The initial cost of installing a condensing furnace is higher than that of a standard furnace, but it will cut energy consumption by up to 4 percent. If possible, install a programmable thermostat, which will save lots of heat and air conditioning at times when you're away from home. A zone control system, which keeps different parts of the house at different temperatures, is another wise investment.

●●● SOLAR POWER

There's satisfaction—and money—to be gained if you produce even a tiny amount of the power you consume. The statistics regarding the cost-efficiency of solar panels are confusing, but any reduction in bills is welcome, and it's silly to let all that sunlight go to waste. The installation of solar panels is costly and therefore a long-term investment, although since we're living in a time of energy crises, solar panels may well increase the resale value of your house. On a smaller scale, you can also buy a number of solar-powered gadgets and gizmos such as garden lights and battery chargers.

● ● ● WIND POWER

Wind farms are popping up all over, but you don't need to live on a hill to benefit from this renewable energy source. Besides buying your energy from wind-power utilities (find them on the Internet), you can also buy small, domestic-size windmills. They vary in size, price, and capacity, providing anything from small amounts for outdoor lighting to most of your domestic requirements. Installing a small wind turbine may need a permit (as well as consent from the neighbors), so be sure to do your research first. Your local government and manufacturers will help you.

● POWER TO YOUR ELBOW

The clockwork radio was originally invented for use in remote areas of the world where no power was available, but the fact that they don't need batteries gives them added eco-cred. Look for windup cell phone chargers, too.

● WATER

Flushing constitutes 35 percent of household water consumption; installing a low-flow toilet uses only half as much water per flush. Alternatively, fill a bottle with water, and place it in your cistern, so that you use less water with each flush. A shower uses less water than a bath. Also, remember to turn the faucet off while you brush your teeth. If you have a garden, collect rainwater by rerouting the downspout to a large plastic or metal tank, trashcan, or purpose-made rainwater barrel, and use it for watering plants. You could install a "rain harvester" on the downspout. This filters the water and diverts it to a barrel or storage tank for use in the washing machine and for flushing toilets, as well as for the garden.

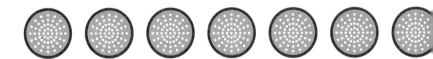

health matters

Thrift doesn't always mean choosing the cheapest; and, where health is concerned, it isn't a time for penny-pinching. With worries about allergies, harmful chemical pollutants, and VOCs (Volatile Organic Compounds), it often makes sense to pay a little more for the healthy option.

● TRANSPORTATION

Transportation is the biggest user of energy, so keep car journeys to a minimum and, where possible, walk, cycle, or get the bus. Cut transportation costs (your own as well as those of retail industries) by buying local produce where possible. Support local stores. You could also join a car-share scheme.

●● BUILDING AND DECORATION

Go for "natural" paints with ingredients made from renewable natural minerals, earth and mineral pigments. They allow surfaces to breathe, avoid condensation problems and are therefore better for both your home and your body. Healthful versions of plaster, flooring materials, and fiberboard are also available, at increasingly competitive prices.

eco-thrift

○ **FOOD**

Grow your own vegetables. If you're not lucky enough to have a garden, you can at least grow tomatoes on a balcony, herbs on a windowsill, potatoes in a trashcan, and zucchini and scarlet runner beans in large pots. If you do have a garden, recycle your kitchen waste to make compost.

●● **FAIR TRADE**

Buy Fair Trade items to make sure that producers get the best price for their hard work.

○ **EXERCISE**

Walking, running, and cycling are healthy activities and are much cheaper than joining a gym.

index